*I must work the works of Him that sent me,
while it is day: the night cometh, when no man can work.*

-John 9:4

Finding Power to Live Ministries® vision statement:

Our heart is to contend for the faith that was first delivered to the Church of the living God. To serve, edify, exhort, and correct that every believer may be more developed into a perfect man, after the image of God in Christ. To see all people gain the knowledge of God and walk after their heavenly callings.

Take a look at my first book, ***Dead to Sin***.

The content of this book is the faith and opinion of its author. No intent was made to judge or criticize another in any way. All names of people and churches were removed to protect their privacy. Thus, no personal information is given. No intent is made to identify anyone. No intent is made to promote Finding Power to Live Ministries® off the back of someone else's success. The content in this book is listed to show Biblical obedience to God, submission to authority, and serving others in love.

Finding Power to Live Ministries® presents:

The Work of GOD

Don't try to change others. Show how Jesus changed you.

MARTIN RAY SUDDERTH

Copyright © 2018 Martin Ray Sudderth.

All rights reserved.

No part of this publication may be reproduced, stored, or transmitted in any form or by any means, including written, copied, or electronically, without prior written permission from the author or his agents. The only exception is brief quotations in printed reviews. Short excerpts may be used with the publisher's or author's expressed written permission.

THE WORK OF GOD
Don't try to change others. Show how Jesus changed you.

Scripture references and quotations are from the *"King James Version"* of the Holy Bible Copyrighted – 1977, 1984, 2001 by Thomas Nelson, Inc.

Additional scripture reference comes from *"The Message: The Bible in Contemporary Language"* Copyright © 2002 by Eugene H. Peterson.

Cover and Interior Page design by True Potential, Inc.

ISBN: 978-1-943852-95-6 (paperback)

Library of Congress Control Number: 2018936193

www.findingpowertoliveministries.com
findingpowertolive@gmail.com

True Potential, Inc.
PO Box 904, Travelers Rest, SC 29690
www.truepotentialmedia.com

Produced and Printed in the United States of America.

This book is dedicated to God my Heavenly Father, His Spirit, and my Savior Christ Jesus. May this book build your life for His glory and give advancement to the kingdom of Christ and of God. I want to thank my wife Kayla and our children; Michael, Amelia, and Audrey. I also would like to thank the rest of my family, friends, and our church for their support of this ministry and its projects.

From the Heart of The Author

I'm excited about the release of this book. While writing, *Dead to Sin*, I kept noticing subjects from my life, which had no place to fit within it. Much of that book dealt with the spirit of Christ and our position in Him. This book addresses having fellowship with God as a Father and the Holy Spirit where it concerns God's work in the kingdom. Much of my testimony has been included. Just as I saw the first book, the name along with an outline for much of its content, I also saw this book presented to me in the same way.

Have you ever wondered why one person is more receptive to God while another may not seem to be? What makes the Christian life seem easier to some, while others tend to struggle with moving into spiritual things? It could be said that some people deal with life better than others. Or perhaps, you may think God gives more favor to one than another. I believe we can find there's more to it than that. I understand no two people are alike and the pattern of our lifestyle is constantly changing. Though that is true, God is constant. He never changes. Having and knowing Him is the one thing, which has brought balance to what was at one time an unpredictable and insecure life.

I probed deep into my past with the intent to uncover an answer to some of those questions. I searched for tipping points where I experienced God. I wanted to know why I encountered Him as I did. I wanted to see what took place, which enabled more change to come into my life. I studied my thought patterns and changes to certain ideas which might indicate moments where I was crossing over. I hoped to pinpoint what it was that could've prompted such occurrences. Though I don't remember all the details, I believe I have recovered enough.

In order for God to change your life, you must allow that change. We must give room for more of Jesus and less of self. It takes being able to see things in a different way. Otherwise, we may not have the potential to know what's coming next or recognize what God is saying and move when it's time to do so. Then there's having the motivation to follow Him to the end.

Is this a statement your familiar with? *"They're on fire for God."* This means someone has experienced personal revival. What a difference change can make. There's nothing like it. I know because I've been there and I've come back not only to tell you my story but also to take you with me as I venture back in. So, follow along with me on my journey. Come with me to the other side. Who knows, you may even find God's hand in your life. Then you will return with a story of your own to tell. May God bless.

Contents

	From the Heart of The Author	7
Chapter 1	**The Work of God**	11
Chapter 2	**Growing up in Church**	16
	Don't limit God	18
	Life should be lived, not dreaded	21
Chapter 3	**Seeking and knowing Him for myself**	23
	7 keys to growth	28
	My crossroads became my crossing over	35
Chapter 4	**My life was becoming an adventure**	39
	My sheep hear my voice	41
	Going in deeper	42
	Knowing God's presence	44
Chapter 5	**Another turning point**	47
	A new seeking time	49
	My first 40-day fast	51
Chapter 6	**Then, He called me by name**	54
Chapter 7	**I could hardly believe my eyes**	59
Chapter 8	**What are you doing to me now, Lord?**	65
Chapter 9	**Wanting more of God**	69
Chapter 10	**Lord, show me you're Glory**	75
Chapter 11	**A new life with new power**	80
	A sense of heavy caution	80
	Something startling	81
	God's hands on your life	83
	More power than before	85
	My last conference	87

Chapter 12	Humility is the key	91
Chapter 13	The spirit of the supply of Christ	93
Chapter 14	Who is on the Lord's side?	97
Chapter 15	Going to another level	103
	You shall receive power!	107
	Elijah must come first	109
	The double portion	110
	Don't bury your talent	112
Chapter 16	The Christ factors	115
	Factor one: Know God's Word	116
	Factor two: Knowing Christ	117
	Factor three: the Visitation	118
Chapter 17	Breaking the chaos	121
Chapter 18	We all have a part in God's work	125
Chapter 19	Formed in life; formed in Power	135
	Live by faith	138
	Walk not after the flesh	140
	God's tabernacle is Holy	143
	Give no place to the devil	145
Chapter 20	Walk in spirit; walk in Power	149
	Dominion starts with Christ	153
	Conclusion	155
	About the Author	159

CHAPTER 1
THE WORK OF GOD

"Then said they unto him, What shall we do, that we might work the works of God? Jesus answered and said unto them, This is the work of God, That ye believe on him whom he hath sent." – John 6:28-29

FROM THE BEGINNING, FATHER GOD PLANNED FOR "THE CHRIST" TO ENTER INTO THIS world. The reason: Salvation. There was no greater purpose in His mind than that. Adam and Eve fell short in following through with His plan for their life, leaving it unfulfilled. So, Christ Jesus was sent; sent to bring back life, truth, and dominion. The ministry of Christ Jesus wasn't for salvation alone. It was also a ministry of establishing the authority of God in the earth once again. That authority is the kingdom of God. The heart of Finding Power to Live Ministries® is about finding His purpose for your life and walking in His power to fulfill it. Through Adam and Eve this position of authority was given over to the devil; but, through Christ Jesus, this authority was given back to us who know Him and believe.

After my attention was drawn to John 6:28-29, I read another scripture describing the work of God differently. In John chapter 9 we're told an account of a man born blind from his birth. The disciples asked Jesus if sin was the cause of the man's condition. In verse 3, **"Jesus answered, Neither hath this man sinned, nor his parents: But that the works of God should be made manifest in him"**. Now, wait a minute. Perhaps you're thinking the same thing I did. John 6:29 stated the work of God was to believe in Jesus as the Son of God. This dealt with God's salvation to mankind. Now we read in John 9:3 that Jesus said the act of healing this man would be doing the work of God. I'm going to be as straight and forthcoming as I can be. For that man to receive healing from God is the same as him gaining back more ground, which was once lost by Adam and Eve to the devil in the Garden of Eden. When Adam lost dominion, mankind gained sickness. Whether someone is healed, delivered, saved, or receiving a blessing; in all of these things we find not only restoration but also restitution of the fall of man.

When I think about restoration, I think of it as dealing with what's going on between you and God. Restitution deals with what's going on between you and the earth. Christ wasn't only restoring the relationship of mankind with the Father. He was restoring the earth back unto mankind. This was something, which was prophesied about from the beginning of the world. Acts 3:20-21 says, **"And he shall send Jesus Christ, which before was preached unto you: Whom the heavens must receive until the times of restitution of all things, which God hath spoken by the mouth of all his holy prophets since the world began."** Here the Word clearly teaches that Heaven (God, the Father) took Jesus and is keeping Him until this work is finished. This is why God gave us the kingdom. When Jesus healed that man the kingdom gained more ground. Strengthening and building God's kingdom is a part of the work of God.

The work of God starts with believing in Christ Jesus. We must believe that He is the Son of God. That He was sent to save mankind from sin, resurrect the spirit man back to life, and restore a relationship with the Father. This is not limited to only salvation. It also includes your spiritual development as mentioned in Ephesians 4:13. **"Till we all come in the unity of the faith, and of the knowledge of the Son of God, unto a perfect man, unto the measure of the stature of the fullness of Christ."** The first part of the work of God that's mentioned is to build the kingdom of Christ (Ephesians 5:5). That deals with developing the body of Christ; the Church of the Living God. The other part of the work of God is to serve and build the kingdom of God. This deals with dominion because God gave authority to Adam and Eve. The kingdom of

God has been here since the beginning. Christ has only been here about two thousand years.

As we examine these verses on the work of God a little closer, they resemble the perspective found in typical modern-day Church. In some circles of faith, almost everything is limited to the work of "The Great Commission." Most of these churches are not thought of as being power churches. They are recognized for their work where salvation is concerned. They are the ones, which teach things like the baptism of the Holy Ghost with the evidence of speaking in new tongues is no longer available to the Church. The other side focuses heavily on manifestations of power like the baptism of the Holy Ghost and physical healing. Many of them are not known for their evangelism to the lost. I understand there are churches, which pursue a balance of both. I have found a few where I live. Yet, most churches fit the description of only one more so than of both. This book has been written to help identify there's a balance between the two. We must have a relationship with God as a Father while walking in His power. Only basing our faith on the knowledge of the Word can make someone religious. Only holding to the power can make someone weird. For believers to walk as the Church was designed, we must have a harmony of both active in our lives.

Serving the kingdom is more than just getting people saved. That's where it starts. Too many believers limit His work to only that. The work of God is anything, which establishes the Church of God (the body of Christ) and the kingdom of God. The work of God is about establishing the body of Christ and taking back the ground Adam and Eve lost to the devil through disobedience. That ground deals with being complete in spirit, soul, and body. It's about more than just what a denomination has previously told us. Christ Jesus said in Matthew 18:11, **"For the Son of man is come to save that which was lost."** Did you not consider He was including everything that was lost? Why should we limit that to only our spiritual life? Is dominion not one of the things, which were lost? Walking in kingdom authority is walking in dominion. Walking in dominion is about the **"restitution of all things."** The Church as a whole doesn't seem to be aware that. If you look close, you can see it almost everywhere you go. I'll give you an example.

It was in 1998. I went to the dentist for my annual cleaning. As I checked in, I realized I had seen the young woman that was helping me at a church I once visited. I asked her, *"Are you still involved in Church?"* She said she was. So I asked, *"What do you do there?"* I guess my question was unexpected. She looked at me like something was crawling out of my nose. It was easy to see that she wasn't sure how to answer me back. Come to think of it, she may not have even understood my approach. She responded to me by saying, *"What do you mean? I....go to church there."* She answered me as if I was asking her a trick question. What she said revealed to me she not only had a limited view of the purpose of Church; but, she had a limited view of the reason for her life and His salvation. It's the responsibility of the Church to teach God's people what our purpose in the kingdom is. Sometimes I wonder if the Church, as a whole, really even knows what that is or what this life's all about.

In 1999, after two years of spiritual growth and transformation, God revealed His purpose for me. It has now become the most important truth for my entire life. It just happened to be contained within a handmade sheet of framed parchment. This artwork held the verse Philippians 3:10. The words as shown on it are, **"That I may know him, and the power of his resurrection."** Located above that verse was an image of a crown of thorns. I hung it in my prayer room over my couch. One day while in prayer I looked up at the artwork. Then, in surprise, I heard the voice of the Lord speak these words. ***"To know Him is to know the image of Him formed in your spirit through salvation. To know the power of His resurrection is to know the power that image holds and what it's capable of doing."*** From that day forth I set out on a journey to discover what this truth meant and do everything I could to be developed in it. This focus has consumed me in every area of my walk with God. Now I've come to see this revelation may be one of the most significant truths for the body of Christ because of two reasons. The first is Christians are formed after the life of Christ Jesus as a living spirit. The second is this life we now have is formed after the power of that same image.

I began to search the Word of God to find a balance between His life and power. The more understanding I find about Him, the more this reinforces the work of both in my life. I am finding it through being a servant, through the study of His Word, and in having a relationship with Him spirit to Spirit. The most important thing we can do is develop an interactive relationship with the Father. To have church without having a relationship with Jesus Christ and the Father will only result in having religion. To follow God properly, the Bible should be present and observed as a part of our life. Every Christian should also develop a service mindset through a spirit of humility. This is where the work of God must begin. After all, it's only normal to want to give back to the Lord when you know the price He paid for your salvation. Everyone should come to the place of knowing God for themselves and seeing that He loves them personally. This knowledge can only be realized through having a relationship with the Christ. This will bring a powerful change in a person's life. When this change starts, finding the desire to serve becomes a part of who you are. You see, the purpose for your life will become real when you allow God to become real to you. By being a servant, studying His Word, and knowing Him personally, you will see that for yourself. That's what happened to me. This was how lasting change began. That's how His power is introduced.

Being a humble servant is vital when doing the work of God. Those that implement true Godly humility won't have to worry about finding the power of God for their life. I can say that because it's quite difficult to do this if your heart and mind have not been prepared properly. Seeking after humility has always been more important than pursuing power. To seek after humility is to seek to have a heart after God's heart. To seek power without the right heart can lead you to the same place Adam and Eve ended up. That will result in losing everything.

> Being a humble servant is vital when doing the work of God. Those that implement true Godly humility won't have to worry about finding the power of God for their life.

CHAPTER 2
GROWING UP IN CHURCH

I CAN'T RECALL AS MUCH OF MY CHILDHOOD AS I WOULD LIKE; BUT, I CAN REMEMBER a little. My early church life, I must say, was respectful and pleasantly traditional. Growing up in church was a normal part of life for me. I enjoyed it about as much as any child could. I have much to give God thanks for. I realize there are many which were not as fortunate. Some people were just not brought up that way.

I grew up in a Southern Baptist Church. I know they were not seen as being on the cutting edge of Christian ministry; but, that house of believers loved one another like a family and worked together. Many of them had a wonderful heart and set a good example. I never saw the church fellowship split apart. As I've looked back on the years of my youth, I can see it not only was a great influence to create a stronger future; but also, it gave me a good foundation for the first few years of my life. There can be no greater foundation than the one, which has been laid down by faith, hope, and love.

There have been many different factors, which contributed to my enjoyment. I looked forward to things like vacation Bible school, Lock-in's, games and craft projects, church wide dinners, different outings, friendships, fellowship, special signings, and the list goes on. God's house was a place where I knew I was always welcome. We were more than just friends; we were family. To some of us, church was our second home. As I look back over the years, I realize growing up in a church was the best thing for my life.

Church association can be wonderful as long as we don't stop there. Life is not supposed to be all about going to church. It involves how we live outside of one. There's more to life than just going to a Sunday service. We, believers, help make up what is referred to as the Church, the government of God in the earth. What church attendance should do for every believer is prepare him or her for what life brings. I'm referring to trials and hardships. Secondly, we are to represent God's kingdom. Yet, I see many aren't taking God and the Church seriously. I don't know how some people can make it in life when God's not involved in theirs. This is the way I see it. If you're not taking church seriously, then you're not taking God seriously. Furthermore, if you don't take God seriously, then you're not taking this world seriously. Don't put your focus on the wrong things. Some people are more concerned about holding on to something from this world than they are with what they're losing because of distractions. This is what our focus should be, *"What have we done with what we've received from God through serving Him and becoming His Church?"* This is why we need to be a part of a group of believers. The church is a place of provision and stability. If you're not getting from God what you need where you are, then pray about moving to another church. There are others out there. Don't just listen to talk. Go and find out for yourself what's going on in other locations. This will always be better than just quitting.

Another reason why I say we need to be a part of a church is because this provides a place for one to fit into the family of God. If the body never comes together then how can they be fitly joined (Ephesians 4:16)? Hebrews 10:25 tells us we should not forsake being an assembly of believers. After all, are we not the body of Christ? The body will function better when all the parts are working together. I know that to be true on a personal level. Besides, the Church is supposed to be running the front lines where kingdom work is concerned. Ephesians 4:12 says it's, **"For the perfecting of the saints, for the work of the ministry, for the edifying of the body of Christ."** There is no "government of God" without there being a church in place. We need church. I think it's sad that church has become a source of hurt for many people instead of a source of help. A bad representation of church is a bad representation of God. If God wants to do anything it's to help His people; not to see them hurt. I think the main reason this has happened is that folks have a tendency to go to church for the sake

> We need church. I think it's sad that church has become a source of hurt for many people instead of a source of help. A bad representation of church is a bad representation of God.

of people instead of for doing the work of God. Yet, there's another problem. Some people are more devoted to this world than they are to God.

1. We need church to help us become spiritually developed.
2. We need church because the world needs God's salvation and what will happen to them as a result of a healthy change.
3. Church will provide direction. Someone has to go to the world with His message. Why not you?

Don't limit God

If your experiences with God have been limited to the four walls of a church building, there's a problem in your walk with God. Some have become so busy working for Him that they forget how to walk with Him. Our relationship with Him should be the center point of everything we know, focus upon, and react to. Building a relationship with God through Christ has built my life. It's all about relationship. Not that I disregard holy living. No. Obedience is a part of relationship. Yet, I've learned that having intimacy is being in right standing with God. I know church is necessary, but life takes place outside of church services, not just in them. Sunday and Wednesday are only two days. What about the other five? How do you live when you're not in church? How do we regard righteousness when you're not with other believers? It's important to know that God's not limited to certain days in the week. God's not limited to a certain place either. You can experience Him in everything if your heart and mind stay right and keep focused. Always be aware of what's taking your thoughts and driving your actions.

What if our actions regarding church is the reason we're limited with God? We're either going to be living for this world or for the Lord. We're either growing in religion, or we're growing in relationship. If we remove relationship all we have left is religion. If we're not careful, our limited view of God can result in limiting God's access to our life. We can make it hard for Him to have the liberty to influence us. Above all, your relationship with God is the most important thing. It's not that church isn't important. There has to be a balance of both. Yes, we need church. However, there are some who have made the mistake of making it all about church. Please don't think I'm contradicting myself. I'm not. What I'm trying to explain is that having church is not a replacement for having a relationship with God. It's sad when people think all they need to do is show up in a service. On the flip side, it's sad when people think they don't need church. That's almost saying they don't need God. You can see God move in your life just as much outside of a church service as you can by being in one.

No one should limit their knowledge of God or Christ to only what they see, feel, and experience in a church service - whether good or bad. I say this because God should be our source, not people. All though I have seen God use others to influence me. There's nothing wrong with that. But, we must learn how to personally experience Him and follow His leading. Now I'm not saying limit your time at church. I'm saying don't limit God because of church or by the way it's been handed down to you. It's about what God is handing down to you personally! We're all different. Take time to search things out. Look for Him on your own. Give it some time. God may pull on you differently than He's pulled me. That's because we all look at things differently. It depends on how your life has gone and where it's taking you. Here's some of what I mean when I say seek Him for yourself. A few years ago a man came up to speak with me after I preached. He said, *"I don't know when I've heard so much revelation given out in one message. How and where did you learn so much stuff?"* I responded before I really thought about his question. I answered, *"By living my life out of my prayer room."* Never limit God to going to church. We are called to be the Church. Some of my greatest experiences have taken place when I wasn't in one; I was at home or at work.

> **No one should limit their knowledge of God or Christ to only what they see, feel, and experience in a church service - whether good or bad.**

A person's relationship with God has both corporate and personal involvement. Corporate interaction provides us a place to learn the truth, serve others, and grow through Godly correction and instruction. When it becomes personal, things change on deeper levels. We all need His personal touch. Yes, there are corporate outpourings. But, in most cases, for one to receive them it must be personal. Everyone must arrive at the place where they are willing to seek God personally for who He really is and for what that will mean for their life. I remember how I felt when I came to my day of spiritual reckoning. That day was a wake-up call for my life. A person's choices can control their direction in life. But, we must take the next step to make the necessary change. Everyone must be willing to learn there's more to salvation than not going to hell; there will always be more to God, His Word, and the life He's given us.

One of the reasons I'm writing this book is because I found out there's more. I arrived at a place in my life where I needed more; much more. The things, which were happening, started tearing me down. Life was becoming difficult. I had to find a release. I didn't want things to stay the same. I needed Godly change. But, what I knew wasn't enough to bring me the change I longed for. Everything that surrounded me was draining my strength. I knew I was being bombarded by influences that were designed to tear me down. Things were not working out for me the way I needed them to. In many cases, it seemed like I was taking one step forward with two steps back. I have known others who felt that way. Perhaps you may be one of them. This is one reason why we need a relationship with God while being involved in a church. No one can handle all that life brings. We need help.

Most people have to *"hit bottom"* before they will turn and rely on God entirely. This is because of the tendency to do it ourselves. Too often we take matters into our own hands. It's only normal to want to fix it yourself. Most people have been raised to think that way. There are some things we just can't fix or control. We will need help from God in doing that. Before this works we must give God our all. Yet, most people are unwilling to make that kind of sacrifice. Surrender is a hard choice to make if your focus is on the world. There must be a surrender of body, soul, and spirit. So, how do you really know when you're giving your all? How do you know if you're truly surrendering? Giving your all happens when you never stop surrendering your life to Christ. Giving your all takes place when you never stop giving. This is something that's done daily. To arrive at the point of truly finding Christ and living for Him, we must be ready to come to the end of ourselves. This is something that only comes out of brokenness and sacrifice. Self-centeredness must die. If you can't find Christ, it's because you're looking in the wrong direction.

Life should be lived, not dreaded

As a child, I attended church fairly regularly. As I grew into teen years, I started withdrawing from church, and from God. Withdrawing wasn't intentional. It just sort of happened. This is something that's easy to do. Life has a way of being busy and distracting. Sometimes when our interests in life change, they have a tendency to change us. At first, it doesn't seem like a big deal. This not only is easy but, it's also dangerous. If something has enough pull to distract us, then it has the potential to change us. To withdraw from church is a step toward withdrawing from God. Withdrawing from God and church can bring adverse changes in a believer's life. This change can start out being subtle, but the negative results won't be.

Think about your life as it is right now. Is it everything you want it to be? Are you in a worse place today than you were a few years ago? Has life become more difficult? Have you ever said something like, *"Sometimes I get on my own nerves?"* Is your life a struggle? Are you mentally or emotionally tired? Does it feel like the things in your life get worse instead of better? Do you get mad when you know you shouldn't? Are your feelings easily hurt? How often do you get offended? Do you dread getting up in the morning? Do you have trouble sleeping at night? Do you lack motivation for your life? Do you feel the only moments of peace you have are when you're alone or asleep? There was a time when I could answer yes to each of these. If you answered yes to any, then you need more of God and more of what He can provide through church. We all need more of His peace, His love, and His power.

No one can control everything life brings. But, God can help us do things we can't do alone. Real problems come when we can't take control over our own life to merely take care of our daily business. If we can't take care of earthly business, how are we going to take care of kingdom business (1 Timothy 3:5)? Stop trying to control others. You should first grow to a place where you find the strength to control yourself. Yes, I know you may not be able to take control over every circumstance you deal with from life, but you should be able to take charge over your own affairs.

Life should be lived, not dreaded. Don't get overwhelmed. Life in this world can pull you down. There is a release. It can only be found by developing a relationship with the Father through Christ. I know this because I found Him for my own life. I want you to know that you too can find Him as well. If you're tired of what this world offers, look to Christ. The Lord is holding life in the palm of His hand. He's waiting for you to take it. Vibrant, abundant, and rich are the only words I can use to describe this life. All He's waiting for is someone to seek Him with his or her whole heart. The Father is reaching out to you right now where you are. He's waiting for you to trust Him. You don't have to be perfect as the world sees it or as church sees it. Just be willing to surrender. My experiences, one in particular, was far greater than I could've ever imagined. It changed the way I looked at everything. It was something I would never forget and never get over.

> Don't get overwhelmed. Life in this world can pull you down. There is a release. It can only be found by developing a relationship with the Father through Christ.

CHAPTER 3
SEEKING AND KNOWING HIM FOR MYSELF

IF YOU WERE RAISED IN A CHRISTIAN HOME OR ATTENDED CHURCH, THEN WATCHING and hearing how people experienced God may be familiar to you. This is a good influence most of the time, but it's not enough. The Bible commands us to work out our own salvation (Philippians 2:12). Everyone has to arrive at the place in life where they receive their own experiences. God has to become a real person to you personally. This knowledge must also be based on His whole Word and not just part of it. No one can tell you to do this or that to know Him. God wants you to pursue Him for yourself. I have seen time and again in the lives of others that this is where real change starts. Everyone's story is a little different because everyone's experience is different. To see Him you must seek Him. The more you seek Him, the easier it will be to find Him. You can even arrive at a place in your life where God will become more real to you than this world you're living in. This started to happen for me in January of 1997. My life as I knew it was turned upside down. Or, it would be better to say it was turned right side up. I would like to share my story with you. But first, let me start from the beginning.

> The Bible commands us to work out our own salvation (Philippians 2:12). Everyone has to arrive at the place in life where they receive their own experiences. God has to become a real person to you personally.

It all began in the fall of 1982 on a Sunday night. I was nine years old. My church was having a baptismal service. I watched what was happening. In seeing this, I knew I was missing something. I wasn't quite sure of what it was yet. So, I asked my mom, *"What are they doing? Why are they using water?"* She whispered, *"That boy got saved; he's getting baptized."* As a child, I didn't know much about God. However, when she answered me, I realized I wasn't saved.

I started asking questions. I remember bothering my parents until our pastor came by to share with me what the Bible said about salvation. For some reason I only wanted him to talk with me. I can remember feeling a strong sense of urgency. My parents weren't sure I was ready. They just wanted to be sure I knew what it all meant. The pastor was leaving the church at the end of the month. The Lord was moving him to a new one. The following Sunday was to be his last day.

My pastor came to our house on Saturday. It was in the afternoon. I was nervously awaiting his arrival. The weather was warm with partly cloudy skies. There was a light breeze in the air. When he arrived we sat under a pecan tree in the backyard. I think I recall hearing a bird singing while perched above us. I remember this because we were using metal garden chairs that once belonged to my great Aunt and Uncle. This was the day the Lord saved me.

As the next few years went by, I wasn't growing much as a Christian. It was like stepping through a door to enter a home without going all the way into the room. I had a gift right before me. Yet, I didn't have enough sense to take God out of the box. I knew I was saved. However, I wasn't living for the kingdom or for God. As a teenager, the things this world offered distracted me. I must say though, whether I was at school, attending Boy Scouts, or just hanging out with family, I can remember that God wasn't far from my thoughts. My problem was I didn't take Him and His Church seriously.

Little by little worldly influences crept into my heart and mind. Unfortunately, as the things of this world became more important, the things of God lessened. My focus on the world began to increase while my focus on God decreased. Through different rejections, a sense of hurt and resentment began to develop. This led to loneliness and depression, which brought negative changes. I was becoming more withdrawn. I started feeling overwhelmed at times. I then began struggling with anger issues and became somewhat rebellious. I guess I acted that way because I thought life was unfair and I wanted to fight back in order to get even. As time went by, I found a way to work through it. I simply put my focus on joyful things, which held a potential to distract me from any sorrows.

Life went on bringing good days and bad. After graduating high school, I lived at home for a few years. During that time, I attended a Bible college. They had off-campus night classes at my local high school. By the fall of 1995, I was not only working a full-time job but, I was taking classes almost every night with one on Saturday. To do this, I had to study every available moment. I was so overloaded I had to count back to my first birthday to remember exactly how old I was. That's when I knew it was time to take a break.

At that time my brother and his former wife were about to have their first baby. They just moved out of their apartment into a larger home. The apartment was a little one-bedroom house near the middle of town. They fixed it up a little, and the price simply could not have been better. So, as they were moving out, I was moving in. At first, things where fine; but, after a few months, the isolation got to me. I wasn't used to being alone. Before leaving home, I'd been around someone almost all the time. You may never know how something like isolation will affect you until you're put into that situation. At one point it got so bad, I began bringing the family dog home with me just for the night. My family suggested I just keep her. I didn't because I knew something else was wrong.

Toward the end of 1996, I watched a horror movie "Interview with the Vampire." I'd heard about it but never seen it. The isolation pictured in that movie was somehow reminding me of my own. Yes, that wasn't a wise choice on my part. I made a lot of poor decisions during that season of life. This was a bad time for me. I wanted to turn to worldly things, as long as they weren't illegal, in an attempt to have change in my life. Life at that time was leaving me with a feeling of being trapped. Soon, I decided to read the book. Though doing some reading was keeping me busy; it wasn't helping. I began to feel the same depression I suffered as a teen was starting to return. I guess I kept to myself too much. Most of my friends from work or school had their own families. I was still single. I knew I needed to get out more; but, that's easier said than done sometimes.

The little house was on the busiest road in town. It was normal to see high school kids continually driving by on the weekends. At one time my friends and I had done the same thing. I often stood by my window and watched.

The memories of high school days long gone would flash before my mind one by one. I enjoyed the times of hanging out with friends and meeting new people. The more I stood watching them pass by, the more I felt life was now passing me by. I felt stuck in my own little world and wasn't sure how to change it, or where to start. That's when it hit me. *"I grew up in church so why am I just standing around and doing nothing with it. Going to church three or four times a week, instead of once, would occupy a lot more of my time. Not to mention, it would be good for me."* I may not have started going back to church for all the right reasons, but God had a plan.

It was now Christmas 1996. I decided to start a New Year's resolution of getting involved in church. I began attending regularly. On the second Sunday night of the New Year, one of the church Sunday school classes started a new Bible study. The pastor asked if someone wanted to stand and give a report on how things went. The Bible study was a twelve-week class. Each week consisted of five lessons that we were to do at home. I began to hear good things about it. The Bible study book was called, "Experiencing God, Knowing, and Doing the will of God" written by Henry Blackaby and Claude V. King.

I spoke with the class leader during the "meet and greet" time and asked when it started. I wanted to find out if it was too late to join. I had only missed one meeting. This week they were doing the first five lessons. I got a book from him that night. I awoke the next day thinking about it. All day long my thoughts stayed on that book. I could hardly wait to get home. When I did, I took my time with it. I took two hours to do each lesson that week just to make them last. My life was beginning to feel new to me again.

As I was saying, I took my time with each lesson. I looked forward to every day and wondered what was coming next. I gave each one a lot of thought and put my heart into it. Your focus is very important. The more I put into it, the more I got out. As I've grown in the Lord I've come to realize, the more real you are with God, the more real He can be to you. Up to that point, my knowledge of God and of Christ wasn't much. Taking that class exposed me to more than I'd ever seen before. As I followed each day, I could see this book held within it a deeper understanding of who God really is, and a deeper understanding of His Word. Being under the influence of a better point of view was making it easier to gain the right focus. The people who wrote these lessons had a different heart and mindset from what I had been exposed to. Slowly this state of mind (and heart) was becoming mine. A desire began to awaken within me that I'd never known before. This was the first time in my life where I wanted to know more about God from my heart and not just my head. It was a spirit-driven desire. Seeking God awoke a hunger to want to spend time in the Word and in prayer. With each passing day, this hunger increased. Every lesson gave me a new direction to take. Little did I know that by doing these things, I was awakening and engaging my spirit man like never before. Now, all I wanted was to experience God for myself.

As the next week went by, I began to see many areas of my life that I needed to deal with and change. I had so many things to confront I wasn't sure where to begin. This was when I started listening to nothing but Christian music. Shortly after that, I began watching Christian television. They both helped motivate me better. This motivation made it easier to start confronting things.

Some things were easier to work on than others: things like tithing and not worrying about money when I knew I should be trusting God. Trust had been an issue in the past. I knew I needed to deal with my fears. I wanted to follow Him more. Yes, things were getting easier but, my battle was just beginning. For example, it wasn't long before I wanted to go back to listening to my old music. I know some people feel most music is relatively harmless. I, however, wanted to take no chances. God knows more about that stuff than we do. I now wanted no part of what my old life could give. Deep down I wanted to go all in with God. Perhaps that's why He was about to move in my life as He did. I was giving Him more room by giving Him more of my life.

> Being under the influence of a better point of view was making it easier to gain the right focus. The people who wrote these lessons had a different heart and mindset from what I had been exposed to.

Seek ye the Lord while he may be found, call ye upon him while he is near - Isaiah 55:6

Most people don't see God move as they would like. That's probably because most people are unwilling to give Him enough room to move. How much ground in your life are you holding back? What's it worth to you? There will always be something we struggle with when it comes to letting things go. That shouldn't stop us though. As time goes by, you'll see many things will be easier to release. The more we let go, the more we will grow. The more we grow the more of God we will know. You may not feel very motivated now; but, give it time.

7 keys to growth

- Be willing to wait! Repentance is essential. Don't become frustrated with slow results. Start with something easy and be consistent. Make a list if you feel you need to. I had one.

- Be real! Your actions may lie to others but, they can't lie to God. He knows your heart. He knows what you're really thinking. He knows how you feel and what hurts you have. The sooner you deal with inner struggles, like temptation, the sooner things will change.

- Stay focused! Don't allow the world to distract you. If this world does distract you, it will pull you down. If we aren't careful hurts and wrong thinking can pull us away from God.

- Don't let go! Keep doing what you know you should do. If you're going to let go of something, let go of the world, not the Lord. If worldly things didn't work before, why would we assume they'd work now!

- Don't give up! Make the investment. With time, you'll see that your interests will change. Then you'll find these "other things" will be easier to release.

- Be patient! Change takes time. Finding change may depend on how much you want to have change. It's something no one can avoid. You can't bypass the growth process.

- Don't be afraid of surrender! Start looking for what you gain not what you think you'll lose. Everyone that wants to know Him has to fight and be willing to die to this world and to self. You can have as much of God as you want. It all depends on the price your willing to pay.

At first, change wasn't that hard. The smaller a bug is, the easier it is to kill it. The bigger something is, the tougher the fight. That's just how it goes. Unfortunately, not everything in life is going to be easy. This world is good at testing a person to find their weaknesses. Some folks are afraid of really knowing who they are and what they really want. What you do at this point will determine whether or not you'll get results. This point in your spiritual growth is very important. This is where more people quit and fall away from God.

As another week went by, I began to see results from the change I was going through. My mood was different, and so was my outlook on life. The grip of loneliness and depression was slowly losing its hold. I couldn't remember when I felt this much peace and joy. My heart and mind could now begin relaxing. Stress was loosening. I felt better every day. Some people think they need a drug to make them feel free. All we really need is Jesus. In Him, I was now finding rest for my soul. I could feel my life being restored. This was something long overdue. Living by myself wasn't bothering me as much as before. I now had something to look forward to when I got home. I was learning how to enjoy life again. I wish I could tell you things kept getting better; but, I can't. As hope continued to rise within me, something else was rising up along with it.

> For some reason, small things, which never seemed to bother me from before, began to get on my nerves. Worry, fear, pride, lust, and greed, along with other things, were now more noticeable.

For some reason, small things, which never seemed to bother me from before, began to get on my nerves. Worry, fear, pride, lust, and greed, along with other things, were now more noticeable. I would be going along doing fine, and without warning, something would happen. It might only be a small thing. It was nothing that might be considered a real problem. Nevertheless, something would begin to bother me. At first, it was only one or two things, as I entered the third week, they increased in number. I felt targeted by these emotions. At other times it was like a part of me was losing the tolerance to deal with what life was handing me. I wanted to give in. I wasn't sure what was happening or what caused it. I'm not sure if others around me knew what I was feeling. I can't remember it ever happening like this before. To me, it seemed like, while the good was getting better, the bad wanted to get worse.

As I grew spiritually, I knew there were things in my life I would have to confront and deal with sooner or later. I didn't know how many there were, but I did know a few. The very core of my soul was being shaken in a good way. Feelings of confusion and conflict were now being confronted by His peace and His presence. This was the result of me facing the areas in my life that needed change. The reason I had so much internal conflict was that the things of the world, which were in me, started dying. It seemed like the same feelings I had as a teenager were trying to revive again. It felt like the harder I fought against them the harder they fought to remain.

At this point, the loneliness that I thought was leaving seemed to return. It was as though this feeling targeted the very hope I held on to in those times of isolation. Now, I was still living alone. I wanted to have a wife but that time had not yet arrived. I continued to stand and stare out of my front window and watch the cars drive by. Watching them brought back more lost memories of past relationships. By this time I was sure that most of them would have started their own families by now. But I had not.

I believe the enemy enjoyed playing with my heart and mind; especially with memories of emotionally based friendships. I also believe this is something we allow. This is why we must control our focus and deal with hurt like loneliness. Carrying these emotions are the same as carrying damage. With each moment that negatively affected me, I found renting a movie or watching one I owned helped. Sometimes I would cook a fancy meal and buy an expensive dessert. I tried to create a private and comfortable world in my little rental house. At times things were okay, but at other times like Saturdays, it was not. In all honesty, I was feeling "edgy." If something was burnt while cooking, I got mad. If I bumped my toe on a chair, I felt like knocking it out of the way. It didn't take very much to aggravate me. Though I wasn't using bad language anymore, I just didn't feel right about my moods. It was like something was trying to push me back to where I came from. I wasn't sure how to pinpoint what it was or how to deal with it. Nevertheless, I held to my promise to stay in church and never overlooked one Bible lesson.

> The thought of surrender shouldn't create a sense of fear or loss. Surrender was about to take me to a place of security. I just wasn't quite aware of that yet.

A few days later, while feeling on the edge more than usual, I decided to visit my parents. I planned to bring the family dog home with me. I hoped some company would relieve the pressure. As I approached my car I stopped. I thought, *"Doing this would be no different than losing the ground I've fought for."* (At times all of us feel the challenge of surrendering to God is too much to take when it's weighted against this world. The thought of surrender shouldn't create a sense of fear or loss. Surrender was about to take me to a place of security. I just wasn't quite aware of that yet.) As I look back on things now, I believe the moments when I chose not to give into the pressure were the times when I was the closest to breaking through. Maybe by giving in, we stop the pursuit. Like choosing to stop running the race. By not giving in we continue to the end. So, I turned around and started back inside with the intent to shake it off.

Over the next twenty-four hours, I felt so discontented that nothing seemed to satisfy me. I was very frustrated, and I hated that feeling. I could feel the ability to control my temper growing shorter. Perhaps you remember times in your life when you sensed your breaking point. Maybe you didn't know how far off it was, but you knew something was coming. In us knowing what is coming has a way of making it worse when it does arrive. I guess that was how I was feeling at the time.

The next day was Saturday. I arose and drank my coffee. After breakfast, I undertook my regular morning weekend routine. After lunch, I found that unsettling feeling was rising up within me again. For some reason, it was more pronounced that day than with other Saturdays. I'd been fighting it for days, so I guess that feeling was from a sense of weariness. I'd started visiting my Grandparents (on my father's side) more often over the past few months, probably because I was now living alone. But, I decided not to go that day due to my mood being so bad. I thought going to church tomorrow would uplift my soul. So, I decided to wait and go then.

About two hours past and I'd run out of things to keep me busy. I was afraid of what I felt as those moments of stillness or quiet approached. I wasn't sure how it might affect me. I was afraid to face it. As I said before, I wasn't content in doing anything. I found nothing was relieving this feeling of being on the edge. By that time, I was ready to do anything that would relieve my heart and mind from it. It didn't matter what it was. As I pulled myself together, I thought I would go to my parent's house for a while. There seemed to be something going on over there all the time. As I arrived, I noticed their cars were gone. I got out and knocked on the door with no answer. I turned to get in my car. I did not want to leave. I did not want to go home.

When I got back to my house, I went in and put on one of my favorite movies. I think I only sat there long enough to eat a small snack before going out the door again. I decided to go see my Grandparents anyway. I thought to myself, they're always home. Upon arriving, I knocked on the door. There was no answer. After a minute or two, I looked around to see both cars were there. I knocked again. The house remained silent. I went around to the den and knocked on the back door. It was no use. They were not at home either. I didn't know it but they were out with my Aunt and Uncle. At that time my face was getting hot from the stress of my blood pressure going up. My heart began to sink, but my temper began to rise pushing me closer to the edge.

As I got in my car, I remember a sense of release came over me. I knew my brother and his family would be at home. My thoughts were, *"Why didn't I think about this in the first place? I could go by, play with my niece for a while, have some supper and that would be the end of it. That would turn out to be a rather fine evening."* When I arrived, I pulled around to the back to park my car. I was met with something I wasn't ready for. You might have guessed it. They were also gone. I almost lost myself completely. These events might seem trivial to you, but to me, it was a major hit. I was so mad that I wanted to punch the windshield of my car. In my heart, I knew something like this was going to happen and that only made it worse. I closed my eyes and took several slow deep breaths. I squeezed my steering wheel as if trying to ring out a wet rag. I was waiting for my emotions to settle down.

What happened next was not expected. I'd been saving money for months to fix the right side back bumper of my car. Sometime before that, I hit something that cracked the paint job rather severely. Around the late fall of the previous year, I had enough money to fixed it. For me at that time money was a little hard to come by. Now, do you remember what I said about my breaking point and me being on the edge of it? I was staring it in the face and didn't know that. To be honest, I was so mad I was almost shaking. I wasn't thinking about anything except what I could feel at the time. I sat there for only a few seconds before backing out. I wanted my nerves to calm down. They didn't. I felt I couldn't take any more. I just wanted to leave.

I was doing everything I could to hold back. My thoughts all morning long were, *"If I can wait until tomorrow, I will make it to church and everything will be fine."* Unfortunately, in this moment of frustration, I caved in and pressed the gas to back out. That's when it happened. I crashed my car into a tree, smashing my bumper in. I could not believe this. For days I was being bombarded with influences that seemed designed to break me down. For me, this was hitting bottom. It was like years of loneliness, anger, and aggravation was coming to a head at once in that moment. I threw my hands into the air and shouted, *"Okay Lord, you Win! I give up!"* NO! I did not do that! It wasn't that way; I was mad. After looking at the damage, I turned my car around to leave. As I headed for the highway, I put the pedal to the floor. In my mind,

I saw myself hitting that road driving like I was in a chase scene right out of a movie. I didn't care if someone was coming or not.

Everyone has moments in life when they arrive at a turning point. Furthermore, every turning point will test you. In one direction you will find a path that leads down the road to a better life. The other turn will only lead to destruction. In one direction, I would have found myself lost. The other way was leading me home. We may not always see our next turning point, but they're there. Being at a turning point was the last thing on my mind at the time. To be honest, I couldn't think straight. I was too mad. All I thought was, *"I don't care if a car is coming or not."* That's when I remembered my decision to turn my life around. After all, what was I going to go back to? I began telling myself, *"That kind of life wasn't working for you then, so what makes you think it's going to start working for you now?"* I felt like I had nothing to go back to. I saw no real value in my old lifestyle. Even if the only lifestyle I lived was one which was out of my own head. Sometimes things can even get bad enough to make us feel that we don't have a choice. Some people think things are stuck as they are and won't ever change. The truth is we all have another option. Things can change. The problem is when we can't see what that choice is or where it will lead us. Some of these choices only end up bringing us into something worse. Unfortunately, we sometimes can't see that until it's too late. So, remember to no longer look at your conflict or chaos as a struggle, you should see it as an opportunity. God can work through anything!

> Everyone has moments in life when they arrive at a turning point. Furthermore, every turning point will test you. In one direction you will find a path that leads down the road to a better life. The other turn will only lead to destruction.

Some people stay at the place of transition too long. Don't linger in the shadow of change. Walk into the light. If you're not careful, you can miss God's timing for your life. This can be why we miss much of what God has for us in life. My experiences with Him (how I come to know Him) were built and reinforced through proper timing. The more of God's timing I find and follow, the more rest, peace, and power I find for my life. Not to mention all the favor and blessings that come as a result of it. If your life is full of chaos, you may be missing God's timing. You should know that God is not the one bringing trouble into your life. He's trying to bring you through it. He's here to empower us to overcome it. Not to fail. Missing God's timing is missing another experience. If you miss out on experiencing God, then you will miss out on the work of God. Yes, we have all missed His timing before. But, the questions we need to ask ourselves are these:

- How am I holding back from God right now at this point in my life?
- Am I at a place of transition and don't know it because my focus is on my situation or on the world around me?
- What if I'm missing God's timing because I do not want to surrender more of my life to Him?
- What am I afraid of?
- Who am I trying to impress?
- Do I think this won't work for me when it has for others?
- What am I still holding on to which is holding me back?

In John chapter 5 we read about the pool of Bethesda. It was said an angel troubled the waters of this pool. A great number of folk who needed healing waited for the waters to be moved. It was accepted by the Jews that these waters had the power of God upon them to heal you if you stepped down into the pool at the moment of the stirring.

God was not the one releasing trouble into my life. It was this world which brought the tribulation. What God was doing was stirring the waters of my life. This stirring was pushing me to my crossroad. All I had to do to receive His touch was to let go of what I was holding on to and reach for His hand.

> "Verily, verily, I say unto you, The hour is coming, and now is, when the dead shall hear the voice of the Son of God: and they that hear shall live" - John 5:25

Are the waters of life troubled around you today? Are you sinking down into the trouble that surrounds you? Don't look at your problems. Look to Jesus. Know that God is there. He's standing by the pool of your life stirring the waters. Now is not the time to withdraw from Him. Don't miss your window of opportunity. If the waters in the pool of Bethesda were being stirred the people had to move down into the pool before the stirring stopped. Otherwise, they would miss their time to receive. Don't miss your time. What if the trouble you're beholding looks like triumph to Him? What if you think you're moving into trouble when you're really moving through it? What if God is stirring the water to provide an opportunity for you to see Him move in your life? What if your conflict is only God's hand moving and introducing change you're not recognizing?

In a moment, I came to myself. I awoke from what was like a spiritual sleep; a sleep that has held me for many years. It was a sleep which kept me from seeing that God was there all the time. I slammed on the breaks. I don't know how long it was I sat there. Many thoughts were running through my mind. The radio was off. I sat there in that stillness. I wasn't moving. Then I looked around and listened, but not for cars. I was waiting for God. My thoughts began to take me back to my little rental house. Then to the Bible study lessons. I was trying to take hold of myself. I had to make sense of things. I was hurting inside from anger and frustration. Yet, I knew the time had come for me to deal with it and face all the lingering bitterness that followed. It was easy to see that it wasn't going away on its own. I was shaking my head saying, *"Now what?"* I sat there waiting. I sat there staring into that stillness. That's when it happened. I heard His voice for the very first time. I heard God's voice in the stillness and quiet of my surrender. I was now in a place where God could have me all to Himself without this world butting in to disturb us. It's tempting to move at the pace this world sets; too tempting. I think God moves at His own pace, and there I was slowing down to His.

I saw a vision. I saw in my left hand that vampire novel. That book was a representation of the life I was living. It was a dead one without peace and without hope. Without the freshness of the spirit of Christ in our lives, we are like the living dead. A pastor friend of mine calls the lost zombies. They may be alive from the outside, but within their full of spiritual death. In my right hand, I saw the Bible study book, "Experiencing God, Knowing, and Doing the Will of God." This book represented Christ and the life He was waiting for me to choose. That's when I heard Him speak to me. **"*If you are going be a Christian then be one. Make your choice.*"** Each book represented a life, and I was walking the fence between the two of them. No wonder I had so much internal conflict. My spirit, soul, and body were being pulled in two different directions. I was being torn apart.

"Verily, verily, I say unto you, The hour is coming, and now is, when the dead shall hear the voice of the Son of God: and they that hear shall live" - John 5:25

My crossroads became my crossing over

As I heard Him, tears were forming in my eyes. It was like breaking a chain of bondage. The life this world handed over was trying to break me down; but instead, I broke through. I felt tired. Encountering His presence that day was like running into a brick wall. Nevertheless, a huge weight was lifted off of me. Do you know how it feels to fight for a breakthrough and finally arrive at the place you were seeking? This is how it felt to me. The feeling was one of release accompanied by an uplifted spirit that had the power to carry me through life's hardships. I can hardly explain it. It was like becoming a new person. It was like getting born again all over again. I now began to feel refreshed and strengthened. My crossroads became my crossing over.

If you ever want to go anywhere with God you too must cross over to where He is. He's waiting for you. He's always there, and He knows where you are. It doesn't matter what you're going through. It doesn't matter what's in your past. It doesn't matter who your family or friends are. All that really matters is what you do next. He wants to offer you a new future. He's closer to you than the air you breathe. He's calling, drawing, and pulling on our hearts. He loves us and wants us to be near Him. All we have to do is stop fighting and follow Him. To do so we must let go of self. I know it's not easy, but it's necessary for change. It starts with putting Him first in your life. If you haven't found Him, it's because you choose not to follow Him and He knows that. If you don't believe, it's because you choose not to believe. Anyone can find Him; but, do you want Him? Are you willing to surrender? You must make Him more important than self and this world. We must make the choice to trust in Him at His Word, and then simply surrender. That's all it takes. If you will try to do that you will find Him. If you give Him your all, you will find that door and cross over. After all, what if the very thing you're holding on to is what's creating all the hurt in the first place? What if holding God's hand is the only way to make "it" let go?

"Take my yoke upon you, and learn of me; for I am meek and lowly in heart: and ye shall find rest unto your souls." – Matthew 11:29

Finally, for the very first time in my life, I was beginning to know God for myself. In finding Him, I was finding power to live. As I put the car back in gear and started to pull out I knew I was different. I can't say I remember much about that night at home. But, that's okay. God, my Father, was with me and now I knew it. I knew I wasn't alone anymore. The experience made me realize I never was alone. I just wasn't looking for Him. I now found Him in that stillness. The isolation I hated so much was now a form of solitude to me. The isolation I was feeling was from emptiness. This emptiness was created by a loss of hope and the memory of broken dreams.

I used the word solitude to describe a new sensation. It was one of peace and rest. All the external influences of this world had no power to stimulate the core of my being as God did that day. You could say I found the Lord just as Elijah found God on Mount Horeb (1 Kings 19:9-13). In all the chaos that surrounded me, I found His voice. I believe He was there with me all the time; surrounding me and reaching out to me. It's funny how you may see things differently after you look back on them. I think He was always doing something to shift my attention from this world. Due to my reasoning at the time, it didn't quite feel that way. As the years have gone by, I can see He really was there trying to love me. He was trying to be there with me and for me. The problem is that I wasn't there for Him to receive it.

> If you ever want to go anywhere with God you too must cross over to where He is. He's waiting for you. He's always there, and He knows where you are. It doesn't matter what you're going through. It doesn't matter what's in your past.

The next morning I noticed the air seemed fresher than yesterdays. My sleep the night before was more refreshing than the air that morning. I awoke energized with an awareness that was new to me. I knew I was saved; but, as I've said, I never took salvation serious until that day. So, I went forward after the morning service when the altar call was given. I fully dedicated my life to Christ from that day on. I made a point to take a stand for God no matter what came my way. I also knew when other times of struggle or failure would come; all I had to do was look for Him with a heart of repentance. God was my hope now. His peace covered me. My decision wasn't made out of an emotional high or low. It was one from my heart and spirit. This time things were different. This time the faith was real.

I want to ask you a few questions.

- Do you see God in your life right now?
- Where are you standing before Him personally?
- Do you want to feel Him near you?
- How much are you willing to push through or let go of in order to find Him?
- What's in your way or what's in His?

Hardships and struggles really can be easier to deal with when He's a part of your life. You must understand I was willing to go through whatever I had to so I could get to Him. I arrived at a point where it no longer mattered what happened to me or what I lost. I wanted the Lord! I found myself at a place where I was willing to surrender. I was willing to go deeper. I sold out! I gave into true repentance. My heart changed that day. My thinking also changed. I made a change of thinking which resulted in a change of direction for my whole life. Have you?

Selling out to God won't be easy. What makes experiencing God so valuable is the change He brings becomes permanent. This is one reason surrender is such a vital part of your walk with God. With real turning points, there's no turning back. I think that's why it worked for me. What if some people miss God only due to their thoughts and emotions being slightly off? As I think back on that day, I could've only been one step away from finding God or finding more failure. What if our greatest experience with God is waiting for us on the other side of one wise decision? What if finding out only comes through selling out?

> Christ must be the center and the core of our life. Our development depends on that.

So, how do you know if you're really selling out? If we can be bought out again by giving our lives over to lust, anger, pride, unforgiveness, doubt, or another type of sin, then there's more in us that we need to surrender to Christ. Keep in mind that I'm not just referring to a mistake someone might make. Growing in God is a lifelong experience. I'm talking about the sin that's taken root in your body or soul that has become a center point for your life. Christ must be the center and the core of our life. Our development depends on that. Look at it this way. If there are areas left in your life which need more spiritual growth, then there's more left to give to God. The devil can always give you what you want. I wanted what God had to give, not the devil or this world. The devil will always be more than prepared to convince you of taking his price. He's the world's greatest con artist.

CHAPTER 4
MY LIFE WAS BECOMING AN ADVENTURE

OVER THE YEARS I'VE LEARNED THAT EVERY ENCOUNTER WITH GOD LEAVES A deposit in you, which will become a part of your spiritual make-up. He marks you that way. At that point, more of Him is living in you by changing who you are within. As for me, there were so many things (from big to small) beginning to happen each day that I would write down. I was keeping a note of each experience in a list. Each event led to opening a door for another experience, like creating a design. It was the little, day-by-day things, which helped me build a stronger relationship with God. I was coming to know Him better through watching how He moved to influence me. After a while, I saw so many subtle influences that my expectations to experience Him were growing higher. Eventually, things developed to where God was moving ahead of my expectations to surprise me. This made it easier to see what was coming from Him and what could be dismissed as circumstances. I began to think He was always planning something. Each event seemed to prepare me for more. I could never figure out what was about to happen next. My life was becoming an adventure.

Before each class, we were given a chance to talk about anything that took place during the week before. There were times when it took me ten minutes to share mine. As each day went by, the number of times God moved increased. Eventually, I came to a record nearly thirty experiences each week. During one such class, another member interrupted me by slamming their hand on the table saying, *"I have never seen anyone experience God like this guy!"* When you've been someone who rarely ever heard from God to becoming someone who hears from Him every day, you'll understand it better. It's hard to explain. You must experience Him for yourself.

Everything that happened was designed by God to awaken the spirit side of me. With each encounter, my awareness intensified. As I grew, I became increasingly sensitive to His Word and His Spirit. Bible verses would seem to jump off the page at me as if they were written just for my situations. There were even times where God spoke them to me. I was seeing and understanding His point of view instead of my own. The Word of God had never been so alive to me before. The relativity of His Word amazed me. I owned a King James Version and a New International Version. I grew to prefer the KJV. Almost overnight it went from hard to read, to being straightforward. The Word fit so many circumstances for my life I would say, *"God is becoming more real to me than this world I'm living in."* My knowledge of God and of Christ was growing in me to a place where spiritual things were starting to become a normal part of my life. I could understand them in a real way. Soon spiritual things became more of a reality to me than this world I was living in. It was at that point where I started telling people my faith was becoming logical. Faith is the logic of God.

> Every spiritual quickening will create a fresh desire for God's Word, for prayer and worship, and for living a life of obedience and surrender.

Every spiritual quickening will create a fresh desire for God's Word, for prayer and worship, and for living a life of obedience and surrender. This fresh hunger for God is what makes us ready for the next place of opportunity. Though life has a way of introducing new hardships, that freshness stayed with me through the years to come. I felt so much freshness I was carrying a sense of excitement around with me wherever I went. It has a way of giving you the feeling of being in love. This freshness comes from having the newness of the spirit (Romans 7:6). This newness was feeding my soul with a passion for more of God.

Romans 2:4 says some individuals do by nature the things contained in the law. This is what I became. Through Christ, my nature changed. I was arriving at a place where I was able to walk by my spirit, not the flesh. God was becoming more than just the Lord of my life. He was becoming my heavenly Father. People began seeing me differently. Most were co-workers. They knew I was attending a church. They observed how I lived. They saw the change. That created an opportunity to be a witness of God's work in my life. Every time something happened, I couldn't wait to tell someone about it. As I did, I trembled with excitement. The first few times I experienced this it made me self-conscious. This manifestation would always start with a trembling sensation. It would affect my stomach. Soon the trembling moved into my hands. Because of being a nervous child I never regarded it very much….at first.

Each time God moved it was systematic. There was an order to the arrangement of things. I began to feel His influences were designed to get in the way of the worlds. I could hardly walk around the next corner without running into God. The truth is God will always be right in front of us in everything that comes into our life. Nothing is hidden from Him. He can and will help bring order into our lives if we're willing to do our part. Our job as a recipient is to seek to find a way to be more receptive to His prodding instead of the worlds. It's an amazing thing to witness the creator of all heaven and earth do simple things to simply attract your attention to Him. God was intercepting my life through simple daily events just to reveal Himself to me through them. I really can't understand how some can say they have never seen anything which has shown them Christ Jesus or God the Father really exists.

My sheep hear my voice

Have you ever heard the Lord speak to you? If so, how do you know it's coming through the Spirit by Christ Jesus and not just out of this world's reasoning? While writing this book I was in a Bible study class where someone young in the ways of the Lord asked, *"How do you know when God is speaking to you?"* Jesus said in John chapter 10 His sheep not only hear but know His voice. There are many different ways in which He can speak to us. His Word is the first place to start. If God is going to confirm anything, it will be His Word. Another important factor that needs to be there is something I can't say enough about; it's your focus. Are you looking for the God of the Word or are you looking for the God that is patterned after what's in your heart and mind? I am of course referring to you looking for what you want to see instead of seeing and knowing who He really is.

Having the right focus is a huge part of finding God. Here may be a good example of focus. I have known friends who bought a car thinking they were the first in town to own one like that. After a week or two, they said, *"As soon as you buy a car like this somebody else has got to have one too."* Just because you never saw that type of car doesn't mean you're the first around to own one. I'm sure this other person's car may not have been the first one in town either.

The reason they didn't notice that kind of car before was they were not really looking for it. This is how it can be with God's voice. If we haven't noticed God, it's because our attention wasn't drawn to Him.

The more you look for Him, the easier it will be to find Him. But, we must make sure we're looking in the right direction. If our information about God is wrong, then our focus will be wrong. An excellent example of this is another religion. Either Jesus is "The Way" or He isn't. In most cases, false information is a result of taking things second hand. Make it personal. What's God handing down to you? I also understand that exposure to church has a way of exposing us to religion. I guess the point I'm trying to make is this. Too many churches are built by someone else's experiences with God. Everyone must have their own experience for Him to be real instead of just religion.

If you're willing to hear what God has to say, He's willing to speak with you. This is proved by how willing you are to surrender your life over to Him when He does speak. It's also proven by another way. Are you doing what you should be doing, or, at least trying too? I don't mean just some of it; I mean all of it. The more self you give up, the more room you will have for Him. Being able to do more will determine where you really stand with God. If you never interact with Him, you'll never notice He's been near you the entire time. It's one thing to be born again, but it's another thing to be in fellowship with the one who saved you.

Going in deeper

By this time our class was done with the Bible study. As the next couple of months went by things began to slow down. I didn't recognize as much influence from God as before. It's like that sometimes. That doesn't mean He's not there. It doesn't mean you're not living right, either. This was a time for me to grow in what I received up to that point. If we are faithful concerning little things, He will give us more. During these times I found myself a private place. This was so I could be alone with Him and pray. It wasn't always a traditional form of prayer. In many cases, I was thanking Him for everything He's done for me. I would present everything back to Him that I could remember. Every time I did I was able to revisit and relive many of those moments all over again. This helped to keep the memory of them as fresh and as real to me as though they just happened. I can remember one of these prayer times very well. It was on my job. I was in the back part of the building where not many people worked. I was sorting through some items to be shipped out. While in prayer I began to sense that trembling rising within me again. This time I wasn't expecting it. For some reason, it was stronger than other times. It was strong enough to stop me from what I was doing. I finally realized this feeling wasn't normal. It meant something. I just wasn't sure what it was yet. However, I knew it was an unction that came from God. I said to myself, *"Why am I shaking? I'm not cold."* Then I thought, *"This can't be the results of feeling nervous because I'm not talking with anyone. Lord, what is this?"* At that moment, He began to speak again and, just as before, it was in an audible form. **"That's my Spirit getting on the inside of you."** This feeling I was encountering was part of the infilling of the Holy Ghost.

That reminds me of the verses found in John 7:38-39. **"He that believeth on me, as the scripture hath said, out of his belly shall flow rivers of living water. (But this spake he of the Spirit, which they that believe on him should receive: for the Holy Ghost was not yet given; because that Jesus was not yet glorified.)"** Speaking specifically to what was happening; I was feeling the presence of the Father in Spirit form. I gave Him what He needed to access more of my life. That sensation was something which was also experienced by my son Michael. He told me after a Sunday morning service that his stomach was feeling funny every time he went to church. That particular day he said it came over him during the time of praise and worship. Then he said it stopped when we left for home. I suppose he thought something might have been wrong with his stomach. He wasn't sure what was happening to him. I knew in my spirit what it was. I never told him much about my experiences until that day. This was new to him. I was waiting for God to do the work first. Then I would join in with His work. I took out my Bible and read these verses to him. I then shared my experience and watched as his eyes begin to light up. I love it! God is awesome! I can never tell what He's going to do next.

> The more you look for Him, the easier it will be to find Him. But, we must make sure we're looking in the right direction. If our information about God is wrong, then our focus will be wrong.

As I kept growing so did my prayer times. I started incorporating music. Most of which was worship. I liked worship music because it seemed to say everything I wanted to say but in a better way. Not all was singing; some was instrumental. Sometimes I would listen while working around the house. One CD, in particular, was soft enough to sleep to. It was songs of old and new melodies consistent from front to back. Some of the most peaceful nights of sleep came during those evenings while listening to it. In addition to this, another change occurred. I noticed my appetite started to leave me. This change turned up around lunchtime on Sundays. I never quite understood it or knew why it happened. I just counted it as a type of fast, which was driven by my new life in Christ. It lasted over two years.

Knowing God's presence

I began taking prayer walks. My grandparents lived on an old dirt road in the country. It was always nice and quite out there. When the weather was good, I never hesitated to slip away. I loved watching the clouds as they floated overhead. I enjoyed feeling the warmth of the sun as it shone on my shoulders and the breeze of the air when the wind blew. I would listen to the birds singing and watch as bees landed on flowers nearby. I even remember the sound of the gravel crackling underneath my feet as I walked. I can't say that I talked with God very much during these times. Somehow I knew that wasn't what He was looking for. I realized that having a prayer life wasn't exactly as church had previously shown it to be. Having perfect words were no more important to Him than perfect actions were. This I knew to be an impossibility. He wanted me just as I was. I never felt like I was "walking on eggshells" while walking with Him. I'm not sure I knew the right words to say in those moments anyway. I know now that words were not needed. He understood what I was feeling and knew every thought that went through my heart and mind. Having the right heart, a heart that wanted Him, was all that was necessary. I soon learned He's drawn to our hunger. Growing through moments like these helped me find out part of what true worship was all about. This was one of the times when I was in communion with God, spirit to Spirit.

> I can safely say that God is always seeking those who seek Him. God will work with whatever we have to give Him. He reveals Himself through those things that are relevant and familiar to us.

Most people say they can feel God in nature. I was experiencing the real Him through it. He always felt close to me when I walked that old dirt road. I may not have been able to see Him with my natural eyes but, just as I could smell the fragrance that came from the flowers, I could sense Him near me. Just like the wind unseen would brush against my cheek, I felt He was using it to touch me. I wanted to absorb every moment. I felt tuned into Him. There, in that place, I found Him once again waiting for me within the stillness. I knew He was near, looking into my heart. Just like a father walking hand in hand with his son; we walked together heart to heart. This may sound strange but, as I was getting to know Him, it was like He was getting to know me. This was one of the things I was doing to help build a relationship with God. Can you picture it? Is this something you can relate to? Have there been times where you experienced God's closeness? It was easy to see He wanted to walk with me. I knew He wanted to be with me. I could tell He looked forward to it. So did I. I could no longer feel much of the frustration that at one time had buffeted my soul so badly. His love and peace replaced it. I wish I could explain how real and beautiful His presence is to me and how easy it was to find Him.

Do you know how to find the presence of God? Do you know when He's drawing near? Even as I was writing this book, I recognize a difference in His presence from day to day. That's no surprise to me. With each memory I report, I find myself able to relive those moments over and over again while building new ones. It's like that with any relationship. You have to make an investment. If you want His power and presence to be renewed in your life, start by revisiting those places where more of Him was being introduced. Re-dig the old wells from your past experiences. The ones who pursue intimacy don't have to pursue power. Now, having said that let me ask you something. How much can you remember? How many times have you returned thanks? You must work on keeping the memory of your experiences fresh and a part of who you are. Every experience we have with God is designed to change our future.

As I have come to know Him more, I can safely say that God is always seeking those who seek Him. God will work with whatever we have to give Him. He reveals Himself through those things that are relevant and familiar to us. That's what He did and is still doing with me. But, we may have to target our focus on anything, which may change around us to find Him. If we don't, we could miss God. Remember, He is omnipresent. The secret to change is surrender. The key to surrender is trust. Every time we give another part of our life to Him we are giving Him the power to work in our life. Is there conflict in your life right now? Every problem you encounter is a door of opportunity to cross over to where He is; or, to allow Him to cross over to you. Don't fear hardships. Take advantage of them instead of allowing them to take advantage of you. Conflict has a way of forcing you into a place that demands change. But, you must be aware of the importance of that change.

You must be willing to deal with whatever this world throws at you. Don't fall for it. You are an over-comer in Christ. In every step we make, if it's not a step of surrender, it may be a step away from God. Who knows, you may even be arriving at a turning point in your life right now.

"Lord, may each person who reads this book pinpoint where you stood before them and where you stand now. Help them to see what you're about to do next. Not just out in the day-to-day circumstances of life; but, while in prayer, in the study of your Word, and in those moments of stillness and reflection. Help them to recognize what's coming from you. Draw their faith to a place of hearing and seeing. May they know the patterns with which you influence them. Draw us deeper to you Lord. Reshape and remold us. Take our attention away from this world. Draw us closer to you. Amen"

CHAPTER 5
ANOTHER TURNING POINT

OVER THE NEXT FEW MONTHS, I SERVED IN CHURCH IN ANY WAY THAT WAS NEEDED. Sometimes I would usher. I also helped my Sunday school teacher do the class. My main focus was on door-to-door visitation with the pastor. There even came a time for me to preach. It was Baptist Men's day. I'd never spoken to a crowd before. Normally, I wouldn't have done it. I was so nervous. Yet, somehow I knew in my heart the Lord wanted me to.

Before I realized it one year had passed. A new year was beginning. I stood in my little one bedroom house and looked around. I thought about where I was a year ago and where I'd come from. I remembered what my life was like and how hard it was. Thoughts of where I would be next year flooded my imagination. I could hardly believe how far God had brought me. I didn't know it but I was about to face another turning point. It didn't come because of a tragedy. This was about a new place and more change. My grandmother (from my mother's side of the family) fell a few months earlier and cracked a bone. After Papa died, she lived alone. So, because of the fall, she was forced to move into an assisted living facility around September. My parents asked before her move if I would consider helping her so she could stay home. I felt too young. The very thought of doing something like that was more than I could handle. I thought I could barely take care of myself. It wasn't long before I was put in a bad position. I was forced to make a decision.

The following week my landlord gave me some bad news. *"I guess you heard that I'm selling off my houses?"* I responded to him the only way I could. *"Ah... No."* He was in his early 70's, I think, and felt he was getting too old to keep up with them. He owned five. The people who were buying mine weren't interested in renting it out. I had just over a month to find another place to live. I wasn't sure how to take the news. I could hardly afford that place. I didn't know what I was going to do about renting another house. As I walked up those steps, I began thinking to myself, *"Now what?"* In all honesty, I wasn't that worried. Somehow I knew things were going to be alright. I'd already seen the Lord come through on several occasions. For the first time in my life, I was learning how to trust God. As I stood in the doorway, I was caught off guard. The Lord began to speak to me. He told me what to do.

Now, when I say God spoke to me, I don't mean I could hear Him in the natural. There are three ways in which God speaks to me. The first way is by reading the Bible. Sometimes God's Word has a way of fitting your circumstances perfectly. Another way is like downloading a program in a computer. It's receiving a lot of information all at once. Then there are times when God has spoken to me with His voice. When this happens, I don't know what's coming next until He says it. It's word for word. It's like having a small speaker installed inside me. The sound I hear is a still small voice. It comes to me through my spirit man. This was one of those word for word moments. Most of the time when He speaks everything around me seems to go silent as though only He is there.

As I was walking into the little house, He said to me, **"This is what you're going to do. Move into your Grandmother's house. Have your mother bring her home. After a while, I will take her to be with me. Then you shall have that house."** Did things happen that way? Yes, they did. My grandmother passed away around nine months later. This wasn't a sad event for me because I knew she was in heaven. I knew God took her. Matter of fact, she died of natural causes. Through the help of my family, and a new job, I was able to buy her house. God can always show us the way. Matthew 6:33 says if we are willing to seek Him and put His kingdom first then all we need will be added to us. How much do you trust the Lord? He knows what you need. If you put God first, you will come out on top in the end. Make no mistake about this. God can provide for His children. God will show us the way. God will keep His Word. All we need to do is believe.

A new seeking time

I was starting the New Year with another Bible study. Sometime the year before, my Sunday school teacher attended a Promise Keepers meeting along with a friend from another church. He brought back with him a copy of a daily devotional. The Promise Keepers divided up the New Testament into one year. He thought this might interest us. In addition to doing the devotional, I was transforming my grandmother's bedroom into a prayer room. I was working on it for weeks so it would be ready to use by the first of January. The room had two windows in it. The side window caught the morning light while the front caught the afternoon light. This was the brightest and most cheerful room in the entire house. Besides, my grandmother was always a spiritual pillar for our family. So, I knew this was going to be perfect.

Though I was waiting for one or two things to finish my prayer room, I had it ready enough. The morning of New Year's Day, I used it for the first time. The room had old hardwood floors in it. It originally was wallpapered, but now it was painted a light pastel tone that would complement the mood I knew it would soon carry. I found a set of stone-like crosses that I hung on the wall. There were seven in all. About that same time, I found a beautiful picture of a nature scene in my grandmother's belongings. I decided to use it because every time I saw the picture I thought about what heaven must be like. Two months later I found the handmade parchment with the crown of thorns embossed in it. I added some music, furniture, one or two other things, and it was finished. I dedicated it to the Lord. The more I used that room, the more of His presence I could feel within. The air seemed to be different in there. Sometimes it was like I could smell a little of heaven. It was like His presence rested in the atmosphere as a lingering fragrance. The air was always fresh, as though God pumped oxygen into the room. I can't describe it. There are no words. Sometimes I wondered if God's presence seemed nearer to me because I made space for Him. I'm not quite sure. There's one thing I know to be true, being in that prayer room always made it easier to find the stillness of His presence. This stillness became a solitude for me that I began looking forward to instead of running from.

During the time of writing the book *Dead to Sin*, I was leaving the house with someone. Backing out, they pointed with a shout, *"Hey, I just saw someone in your prayer room. They walked across…right by that front window."* I had just come out, so I knew there was no one inside. I turned saying, *"What are you talking about? There's nobody in there. I just came out."* Then they said, *"Look…I just saw someone walk by. It looked like they were wearing a white shirt or something."*

Was that an angel or the Lord? I didn't see it myself but, this person said that they thought they saw someone. All I can say is this, being in that room was like being somewhere between heaven and earth. It's my secret place. There's nothing like it! It was in my prayer room where God made preparation for much of the change in my life. Nothing can help activate what's in your spirit more than the time you have when you're alone with Him. If you never "lose yourself" in His presence you may be missing the one thing you need the most in life. I said, "lose yourself" because; I'm referring to the parts of our life that belong to this world or is still in need of being transformed. Some things only let go of you when He comes around.

I always felt the presence of the Lord in a stronger way when I was in my prayer room. But, I still wondered if it was something tangible or just in my head. The day soon came when I received an answer to that question. My brother asked if it would be Okay for my nephew to stay over for the evening. He was five years of age. When they brought him by a strange look came over his face. He had a question he wanted to ask me. You must first understand that I was in my prayer room for a while. I wanted to spend some time with God before he came over. I didn't expect he would care for that at his age. Well, I was wrong. Sometime before this, I installed speakers in the ceiling throughout my house and ran the wires from my prayer room. I wanted to carry the same atmosphere into the rest of the house. I had just come out and left the music playing. He looked around trying to find out where the sound was coming from. He then looked at me and said, *"Uncle, you sure know a whole lot about Jesus and the Bible. How come you know so much?"* I said it was because I pray and read the Bible while spending time with Him. I then asked if he wanted me to show him. Without any hesitation he said yes. I took him in and began to lead off in prayer joining him in where I could. Soon he became quiet. It was about this time that I looked within myself and asked, *"Father, I've lost his interest, haven't I?"* Then I saw a weird expression on his face. I didn't know what it was about. I asked, *"Are you okay?"* He shook his head and said no. I couldn't tell if he had a bully at pre-school picking on him, a stomach pain, or something worst. I didn't know what it could be. He then, while struggling to speak, began to say with tears forming in his eyes, *"Uncle, I feel like I'm going to cry, but….I don't know why?"* I did not expect that from someone his age. This wasn't something he was taught to do. This was an encounter with God. I then knew the atmosphere in that room was real. It wasn't my imagination. Jesus was there. To this very day he still remembers everything that happened. It's just as real now as it was for him then. Soon I learned His presence isn't just something we encounter while in a church service, a prayer room, or just throughout the day. His presence is something we carry. It's not about where we go. It's about who we are. His presence is something within us. We are His temple. We are the Church. Allow me to ask you a simple question. When was the last time you felt the presence of God so strong that it scared you?

My first 40-day fast

Ever since God began taking hold of my life I experienced more of Him than I ever thought possible. I don't remember church ever describing salvation this way. It wasn't all about what I was or was not to do. It wasn't only about what God did for me. It was about His love. It was the fact that He was doing something with me; that something was really happening. It was about what I received from the Father personally. It was the fact that I was getting more of Him; that He wanted me to know Him more. This interaction was bringing more freedom from sin than I'd ever known. His influences were so strong at times "those things" would seem to simply fall off of me with little to no effort at all. The more of Him I found, the more power I found to live. The experience of being around Him was changing me from the inside out. I was learning how to walk in victory by learning how to walk in the spirit of Christ.

> I always felt the presence of the Lord in a stronger way when I was in my prayer room. But, I still wondered if it was something tangible or just in my head. The day soon came when I received an answer to that question.

As March approached, I found myself in a new place before God. He was demanding something more of me. Something I'd not been able to deal with appropriately up to that point. There was a sin in my life He now needed me to face. Do you remember what I said about the bigger something is, the tougher the fight? Well, something was fighting against me; something big.

The root of it was buried deep within my soul. It's influence came to me as a small child. I'd been caring it for many years. I hated it but, I didn't know what to do about it. I'd been more aware of it since God arrested my soul back in January of 1997 with little results. I needed some help; so, I called a friend. To this very day, we're still friends. I knew I could trust him with this information. I decided to go over to his house. It was Saturday, March the 6th 1999.

He answered the call to ministry a few years earlier. He lived just up the road from me. He was attending a Bible College in the Northeast Georgia area. There was another friend which God used as an influence for my life. They both were friends for some time. At times, as I drove by my friend's house, I would see them outside talking. He was also called into the ministry. As I think about it, there was another man of influence in whom I had come back into fellowship with which was also called by God. Over the past year or so, there were several times where we had the chance to fellowship together also. It was strange that all the friends (the one's God brought into my life) were called to ministry when I wasn't. Little did I know that my time for God's call was about to come.

On that Saturday, I called him up. I had just driven by and knew he was home. We sat and talked for a while at the kitchen table. Then we prayed. I shared as much as I could with him. He knew what I was going through. He said it was only a few years before this when he defeated the same type of struggle in his own life. He then asked if I'd ever fasted before. I said, *"Not as you're talking about, I haven't."* To tell you the truth, I wasn't sure if fasting would help. I knew very little about it. Fasting wasn't something that was often taught in my home church. It was only mentioned from time to time. However, the more we talked about it, the more I realized food wasn't the problem. I said, *"If something contributed to my weakness it wasn't food, but television."* He looked up at me and said, *"Well then, fast your television."* That was like a light bulb coming on over my head. That was it. I could see this helping me. I walked away that day being motivated by a form of logic that I knew was coming from God.

The next morning I awoke ready for my fast. I must say, something was missing, and I knew it. I wasn't really sure what it was yet. I knew I needed to do this. I knew my need for more freedom was stronger than my desire to watch TV. I also knew this would be difficult. Much harder than a normal food fast. When you live alone, a TV can be a big help when it's too quiet around the house. Nevertheless, as I was getting ready for church, I decided to do the fast. After I did my devotional, I thought watching only Christian programming wouldn't be so bad. After all, most of it was preaching anyway. This might leave a bigger door open for God to speak through. I noticed the preacher on at the time was teaching about 40-day fasting. He began to cover some of the same things my friend shared. All at once, the Spirit of God came over me. This reinforced the logic that came to me the day before. I received the full motivation I needed. I decided to do a forty-day TV fast. All I needed was a word from God to confirm my fast and give me the confidence I needed to fulfill it. I knew I had God's attention. Or, rather God had mine.

This is the confidence that we have in him, that, if we ask anything according to his will, he hearth us: and if we know that he hear us, whatsoever we ask, we know that we have the petitions that we desire of him.
–1 John 5:14-15

CHAPTER 6
THEN, HE CALLED ME BY NAME

SOON ONE WEEK HAD PASSED. IT WAS SUNDAY, MARCH THE 14TH. I WILL NEVER forget what I saw that day or what God said to me. This day was going to be the beginning of change for my life unlike anything up to that point. There have been many experiences before this that marked me. None was as powerful as what was about to happen. This touch was an introduction to a new place in my walk with God. It brought me to another turning point. Much of what I learned for the last two years centered on Christ. Now I was crossing over to the ways of the Spirit of God. That morning as I sat drinking the rest of my coffee, I began to read my devotion for the day. The reading was found in Acts 19.

And it came to pass, that, while Apollos was at Corinth, Paul having passed through the upper coasts came to Ephesus: and finding certain disciples, he said unto them, Have ye received the Holy Ghost since ye believed? And they said unto him, We have not so much as heard whether there be any Holy Ghost. And he said unto them, Unto what then were ye baptized? And they said, Unto John's baptism. Then said Paul, John verily baptized with the baptism of repentance, saying unto the people, that they should believe on him which should come after him, that is, on Christ Jesus. – Acts 19:1-4

As I was reading this, I saw the written words of John the Baptist like a voice flashing through my mind. This wasn't God's voice, I think, but a memory of the verse Acts 11:16. I guess you could say it was the thoughts of my spirit more than that of God's. After all, I was reading the Word. This was the information that was given. **"John indeed baptized with water; but ye shall be baptized with the Holy Ghost."**

I was raised in the Baptist Church. We, as a congregation, knew of and understood John's baptism. After all, that's what we were; Baptists. The baptism of water is an outward expression of our death to this world and our resurrection to a new life in Christ. The baptism of water is a baptism of repentance because of salvation. This symbolizes two things. First, it symbolizes the death to our old self through being buried in the likeness of Christ Jesus, then being resurrected with Christ in the act of being baptizing (Colossians 2:12). Secondly, it symbolized the washing away of sin through the shed blood of our Lord and Savior. Do you remember in 2 Kings 5, when the prophet Elisha told Naaman to go and dip seven times in the Jordan river? This was one of the things God commissioned John the Baptist to introduce. It was a shadow type of salvation to come.

As I was reading, I saw something that made me choke. My soul was being arrested once again. I froze and was afraid to move. My reason was hit so hard it took me a minute to gain my focus. As I read, I could see the Apostle Paul attaching the baptism of water to the very act of receiving salvation through faith. The very reason for him doing this was to identify this type of baptism was only a symbol of salvation through repentance. At that moment God gave me the ability to see myself in the same place as those disciples were. I too had learned much about Christ but little about the Holy Ghost.

> The baptism of water is an outward expression of our death to this world and our resurrection to a new life in Christ. The baptism of water is a baptism of repentance because of salvation.

It's hard to describe how I felt. It was like tearing apart two boards after being glued together. This wasn't a separation from God but, a change in where I was in my walk with God. I felt God tear away my old thinking about this truth. I also felt more of self, which this world introduced being torn out of me. I saw that I was gaining Him instead of religion. I saw there was still more of God to push into. I was being positioned in a new place in my spirit. There are some things only God has the power to tear out of your life!

When Paul asked them what baptism they received, he was identifying the baptism of the Holy Ghost. Not the baptism of John with water. He knew they had that. The way in which Paul presented these baptisms separated them as being two different baptisms (Matthew 3:11, Acts 1:5, Acts 11:16). For years all I heard was God would give you His Spirit at salvation. I know that no one can come to God unless His Spirit draws them. But, the bottom line of this truth is you don't get the Holy Ghost at salvation. You get Christ Jesus. Allow me to tell you why. Having a "living" spirit man is having **"Christ in you the hope of glory"** (Colossians 1:27). This is not a spirit born of Adam unto spiritual death. This spirit is now born of God through Christ. The Apostle Paul referred to this as the spirit, which came from Christ (Romans 8:9). Paul didn't say it was the Holy Ghost in you the hope of glory. In addition to this, he also said, **"God sent forth the spirit of his son into our hearts"** (Galatians 4:6). Salvation is getting Christ, not the Holy Ghost. Gaining a new nature at salvation is different than being anointed with the power of the Holy Ghost. The Holy Ghost isn't a son of God. Your salvation is what gives you son-ship. Just because someone is in fellowship with God through the spirit of Christ does not mean they are walking in God's power. (I'm not saying you can't have both given at the same time. That has happened). I have come to see through everything that has happened up to this point that God works on a level higher than traditional church. Some churches don't always present the Jesus and the Spirit of God as found in the Bible. They present the Jesus and the Spirit of their church. As for me, I wanted the Biblical spirit of Jesus. I wanted the Biblical Holy Ghost. I wanted the truth. I wanted real power.

I sat there not knowing what to do. I was shocked. I wasn't quite sure what it meant or what to do about it. It was like getting lost without a map. Everything seemed to happen in a moment. I didn't know how to react. How does someone answer something like that and what do you do in response to it? I'd been a Baptist my whole Christian life. In a second my life was put on hold. God was pushing one of my buttons; the pause button. I can remember it like it was yesterday. It shook me up. I stared at my Bible lying open over my lap. After a few seconds I asked the Lord a similar question as I've asked before. *"What are you doing to me now?"* That very moment, while sitting in my grandmother's rocking chair, I heard the audible voice of the Lord. *"Marty, you have no power. You need my power. You need to be baptized by my Spirit."*

This power God referred to is what He gives us by His Spirit. He wasn't saying that you have no Christ in you unless you're baptized in the Holy Ghost. This isn't dealing with our salvation or our son-ship. The baptism of the Holy Ghost is not what gets someone in heaven. If you read my book *Dead to Sin* you would see scripture that identifies the power of Christ differently from the power of God's Spirit. There is a power that comes to us through salvation. 1 Corinthians 1:24 teaches that Christ is the power of God. So, what was God saying? There is a power that only His Spirit can give us. This power is many times referred to as the anointing.

I sat there silently. I felt God in the room with me. I wasn't feeling fear though. I was feeling a type of security deeper than I'd ever known. Think about that. He is the God of all heaven and earth. He is the one who has watched over each of us from the day of Pentecost until this present time. The one who talked to Abraham, Moses, the prophets of old, and the Apostle Paul was now talking to me and calling me by name. I could hardly believe it. I heard Him call my name.

I can't remember if I finished the rest of my lesson or not. I was too shook up. But, I do recall what I was thinking. I knew there was no one at church that could help me with this. My thoughts were, *"There is no telling what my friends would think or say if they only knew what I just heard."* After all that, I really wasn't concerned about what others might think. I just didn't want any of this to hurt them for finding out what was learned. After pulling myself together, I realized I needed to talk to someone. There were simply too many questions I needed to ask. I didn't think my friend would be the right person to go to because he was a Baptist like me. I finish getting ready for church. That's when I remembered I did have a friend to ask. She attended a Church of God where the baptism of the Holy Ghost was taught and believed.

In a few days, I made contact with her. As we talked, she began to direct me on the right path. She suggested I call her pastor. We arrange a meeting. I told him about what God was doing since the first turning point back in the start of 1997. He began to share a few stories of how God moved in the lives of others in his congregation. He handed over a list of scripture verses from the Bible pertaining to the baptism of the Holy Ghost. He recommended I simply put my trust in the Word of the Lord. After praying, he welcomed me to wait on the Lord at the altar.

Things were kind of quiet over the next couple of weeks. Time seemed to go by very slowly. Not much was happening. To be completely honest it seemed too good to be true. But, I never lost the sound of God's voice echoing throughout my mind. I made sure to hold on to every word. To encourage my faith I visited that church once or twice as I waited for the Lord to fulfill His Word. I hoped visiting might provide an extra push in the right direction.

More encouragement came through the preaching and teaching of the Word. For over two years I'd been watching Christian programming. I observed certain ministers with much curiosity. One of them was Benny Hinny. I don't mind mentioning him because he often talked about how Kathryn Kuhlman was a powerful influence in his life. It turned out that Benny Hinn would soon be holding a crusade in Greenville, South Carolina. I asked my friend if she knew about it. She not only knew but, she and her mother had already made plans to go. The meetings were held on Thursday and Friday, April 15th and 16th. April the 15th turned out to be day 40 of my fast. This changed everything. I knew I had to be there. This could not have been an accident. The timing was too perfect. I knew more change was coming.

At one point April the 15th seemed as though it was never going to arrive. This tested me. My whole focus was on this one thing. Get yourself to those meetings. This was the next thing I knew I could do which would strengthen my faith. It was the next step I knew to take. The fact that God was confirming these meetings was also giving me a knowing that this would be a pre-arranged point of contact for another encounter. Yet I found my faith being tested. I had to work at keeping my faith focused. Doubt was present. Wrong thoughts challenged my confidence. But, His Word always brought me back to a sound mind. I'm not only referring to the Word of God. I was holding on to the word He spoke to me that morning back in March. You see, the Word of God is full of many promises. How many do we really believe? It's one thing to just read about something. It's another thing to know the promise belongs to you! I wasn't just reading a verse. God gave it to me. I'd been called out on it. This truth belonged to me. It was more than hope. It was logical. The Word will become truth that produces when it becomes logical to you.

CHAPTER 7
I COULD HARDLY BELIEVE MY EYES

BENNY HINN WAS FAMOUS (OR SHOULD I SAY INFAMOUS) FOR BEING KNOWN FOR healing and people falling under the power of God. I would watch him on TV. All I could do was wonder. I was told I watched such a program as a child on Sunday mornings before church. I was also told I would put my hand on the heads of people at church and say, "Be healed." It's funny how things sometimes turn out.

I learned in most cases before you can hear from God through them, you must first hear from God about them. Secondly, if you can hear from God through them, you can receive from God through them. This was how I got passed the man to reach the Master. This also worked the same with many Christian books I'd bought. In many cases, I said to myself, *"If this thing doesn't get any better, I don't think I'll be able to finish it."* I have bought and started reading many Christian books; but, I have only heard from God through four of them. The reason for that is because God only spoke to me about these four. I have already mentioned two of the four in this book. First, there is the Word of God. The Bible study book, "Experiencing God, knowing and doing the will of God" was second. The third one was a book Benny Hinn wrote; "Good morning, Holy Spirit." The fourth book is being mentioned later on in my testimony. Going past the man or woman is key to drawing from the ministry. For hearing and hearing the Word is what brings about and builds our faith. The building of one's faith is building on one's knowledge of God. This is something I have seen repeated on numerous occasions. Now back to what I was saying. This was my time and opportunity to see for myself if this show was real or fake. I wanted to be sure. I could hardly wait. My expectations were growing daily.

We arrived early for the evening meeting. It was a little after lunchtime. Hundreds already seemed to be there ahead of us waiting in line at each door around the stadium. It was an amazing sight to see the faith of so many people gathering together all in one place. I'd never had a chance to be a part of something like this before. When the time came for the doors to open, people rushed in like a tidal wave. It didn't take long for the front part of the auditorium to fill up. We sat about two-thirds of the way back in the upper part of the bleachers. This was as close as we could get.

> When the time came for the doors to open, people rushed in like a tidal wave. It didn't take long for the front part of the auditorium to fill up.

The meeting was awesome. People were saved, healed, and the power of God moved. So many of us have either read the biblical accounts of God's power or heard about them from preaching. This was the first time I saw a concentration of God's power on display. Toward the end of the meeting, my friend's mother was watching me. They both knew the word God give me. She could tell something was bothering me. As the meeting was coming to a close, she suggested I not worry about what God did for other people. *"Your time will come. Just be happy for those who have received from God."* As we were leaving, that feeling of not being worthy returned. My faith was struggling. I knew I was allowing things to bring me down. I always second-guess myself to much. With a stern look, she said, *"What's wrong with you? You know God spoke to you. That's more than some people ever get. Just trust the Word God gave you. He will do it. After all, there's still tomorrow."*

I awoke the following morning ready to go. As I thought about the meeting from the night before, I realized everything was fine. I just finished my 40-day fast. That encouraged me. We arrived at the stadium earlier this time. Crowds were already forming at each door. Inside, the morning service was still in section. I don't know how long we waited outside to get in. It was several hours. As the doors opened to receive us, we pushed in with the crowd. Before I knew it, my friend squeezed through the people. We lost sight of her. Her mother and I moved quickly towards the front only to find the seats were filling up fast. To be sure we got a good seat, we turned back to a section nearly halfway down. While picking our seats out, we heard her daughter call us. We saw her up toward the front. She was in a section of bleachers right in line with the stage. She ran on ahead of the crowd and saved us both a seat.

The power of God was moving in a stronger way that night. So many things were happening that I can't remember them all. What I do remember was seeing God's power moving on young people, like my friend and I, in an unusual way. At different times Benny Hinn would stretch forth his hands and pray for entire groups of people. In doing this, nearly everyone would feel the power of God like a weight coming over them and fall back to their seats. All I could do was sit there and marvel. I'd seen this on TV, but now, I saw it with my own eyes. These were people just like me. So, I knew there was something to it. It wasn't too long before he went over and prayed for another section with the same results. The next thing I knew he was looking at our section saying, *"Get ready, you're next."*

Before I thought about it, he was in front of us. He called out, *"Stand up and take the hand of the person in the seat next to you."* As we did this, I closed my eyes. I wasn't only holding the hand of my friend, but I was holding on to the words the Lord spoke to me. Then Pastor Hinn began to pray. I opened my eyes and looked down to where he was standing. I wasn't going to miss anything. He then shouted, *"Goes the anointing!"* The power of God hit the crowd. It hit about five rows up like throwing a boulder into a pond of still water. The anointing spread as a wave moving in all directions. Wow, is all I could say. As it moved it covered the crowd coming in our direction and it was coming fast. I remember saying to myself, *"I'm not closing my eyes. I'm not going to miss anything."* Fifteen rows in front of us soon turned into eleven. Then eleven rows turned into seven. Seven then turned into three. Before I knew it, the wave was hitting the people right in front of me.

I'd been waiting on this to come for weeks, and it was finally happening. It's hard to explain that moment. It was like what someone might feel just before they had a head-on collision in a car. But, this wasn't bad; no, this was something good. I'm merely relating this experience was a shock to my normal

> At different times Benny Hinn would stretch forth his hands and pray for entire groups of people. In doing this, nearly everyone would feel the power of God like a weight coming over them and fall back to their seats.

way of thinking. It was like being in slow motion. Many thoughts seemed to go through my mind. Only one stood out. The words God gave me. I could almost hear them once again as though it were Him speaking to me. *"Marty....You need my power. You need to be baptized by My Spirit."* That's when the power hit me. I felt a force go through my body. It made me shake all over. The weight of God's power took my legs out from under me. I fell back into my seat. As I pulled myself together, I noticed my whole body was shaking and not just my hands. I began to look down at them, *"Is this that same power I've felt for near two years?"* This flow that I'd received from God was like a jolt of fresh energy. This was the same sensation I'd been feeling, only it was much stronger. I knew this was from God. This wasn't just a show; this was real.

> That's when the power hit me. I felt a force go through my body. It made me shake all over. The weight of God's power took my legs out from under me. I fell back into my seat. As I pulled myself together, I noticed my whole body was shaking and not just my hands.

As the service headed into its climax God's power increased. In one section of seats on the floor, which was in front and to the left, several young people began to fall under the power of God. Benny Hinn wasn't near them. But, when he saw this, he left the stage and ran into the crowd. He began praying for them. All eyes were fixed on the youth. Just then he heard something. In turning, he saw another group being touched by God in the right section. If I were him, I wouldn't know where to turn. He ran back on the stage and called out, *"I want all the young people to get up and come down here so I can pray for you."* I was out of my seat and halfway down those steps before you could say "Glory to God!"

My friend and I pushed our way in while others pressed in with us. It looked like we were only 20 feet from where Pastor Benny was standing on stage. He looked everyone over and said, *"Take the hand of the person next to you and raise it up to heaven."* (I have to say I knew the impartation that came earlier wasn't the baptism of the Holy Ghost. I'd felt that for two years. I knew there had to be more and this was my chance to take it.) I closed my eyes and shut everything out; including Benny Hinn. Now, there was only my Heavenly Father. My mind went back to that day: to the very moment where I was alone with Him and heard His voice. I began to take the Lord back to the place where He took me. As I prayed, I reminded Him of His Word and said, "*Lord, I need your power. Baptize me. Baptize me.*" While I was doing this, I was interrupted by something I'd never felt before. My heart seemed to swell and burn with heat within me. I found it hard to breathe. I then said, "*Now what are you doing to me?*" The pressure continued to increase. Then I heard Pastor Benny shout, "*Goes the anointing!*" Whatever it was that filled my chest exploded inside of me running throughout my entire body before releasing through my hands. I fell to the floor.

Everyone that was up front was down. It was like God wanted to play a game of dominoes, only He was using real people for it. A few months later Pastor Benny's TV program, "*This is Your Day*", aired the event. I had to see it for myself. It was quite a sight to behold. The experience was real and no longer just a show. I was a part of it. I'll never forget it. Walking back to my seat was a little tough though. I was shaking all over. It was difficult not to trip. I was high and tipsy on the power of God. This time the power felt different from other times. This had to be that power. This had to be the baptism of the Holy Ghost.

Around five days later I stopped by to visit with my parents. I looked over and saw the neighbors were out on their back porch. I walked over to say hello. As we talked, I looked for an opportunity to tell my story. I soon found out that one of them experienced God's healing touch in their youth. He was at an Oral Robert's tent meeting. This neighbor was born deaf in one ear but was miraculously healed. I knew when I heard that, I had a captive audience. I went through each detail of my experience from the week before leaving nothing out. In coming to the end of my story, I was met with a strange sensation. It started at my fingertips. In seconds this tingling spread throughout my hands. It almost felt like electricity. This feeling was like the pricks of little needles were sticking me. You know the feeling that's in your hand or foot when it falls asleep. It was so strong I felt as though every cell in my palms were vibrating individually. It was like each of them was given a life of their own. I looked down to see if my skin was crawling. I remembered the power God gave me while at the crusade and how it left my body through my hands. I guess that may have been something the Apostle Paul felt. That maybe why he would lay hands on others. Wow, what a power!

CHAPTER 8
WHAT ARE YOU DOING TO ME NOW, LORD?

IN THE DAYS TO FOLLOW I READ THE VERSES GIVEN TO ME BY MY FRIEND'S PASTOR again. I noticed the baptism of the Holy Ghost introduced the gift of speaking in tongues. This was unknown to me. Our Baptist church believed this kind of baptism was only given back in the days of the book of Acts. But, are we not still in those days now? We're now here in the Lord's stead, right? Has the rapture come for the Church already? The more I experienced, the more I wondered how much more remained. So, I continued to pray and study to complete my task of taking hold of the fullness of the Spirit.

A month had passed. One afternoon, when driving by my friend's house, I saw him outside talking with the one I previously mentioned. I pulled in to see them and stayed to talk. Slowly I dropped subtle hints to see if I would have the liberty to share what God was doing in my life. I was testing the waters to see if my experiences would be received. I was looking to see what the Spirit might be doing. The man my friend was talking with took the bait. He also was having questions. He had recently visited a charismatic Christian church where his family attended. He told me he knew there was more and suggested I visit that church with him sometime. I wanted to go yet wasn't sure what to expect. He pointed out how God's power was different there. That's all it took to convince me to go.

It was a new beautiful modern style church building. There were no pews like in traditional church settings. They used padded chairs, and the place was packed from the front row to the back. My first memories of that church were unusual ones. The air was filled with high energy and so was their guest speaker. As he preached he would grab the hand of someone near him and shake it wildly. As he did this, they acted like they were hit with a force of power. Not all of them fell down though. Some looked like they were having fits! It was just a little too much for me. After all, I was only a Baptist. I said to myself, *"Lord, help. You've got to get me out of here."* Just sitting there was awkward. Before I could do anything, the minister walked over to where we were sitting. He came so close I could almost see the color of his eyes. God was doing so many things in my life I was afraid he might sense something and try to grab me too. So, I opened my Bible to look like I was reading hoping this would appear as a distraction on my part. Then I noticed he moved away heading to the other side of the room.

> As he preached he would grab the hand of someone near him and shake it wildly. As he did this, they acted like they were hit with a force of power. Not all of them fell down though. Some looked like they were having fits! It was just a little too much for me.

I wasn't sure about how I was feeling at the time. I wasn't sure about this place. I didn't feel the anointing. The last big experience I remember having was back in April after the crusade. That was two months before this. I didn't want him to pull me out. What if nothing happened? Right at the end of those thoughts, I looked up to see that man coming towards us. I knew he must be coming for me!

In looking up, I watched him walk in closer than before. This time he was only a few steps away. I grabbed my Bible again and let it fall open. It didn't matter what part it was opened to. The first time he stood by us I didn't read it, but this time, I did. I wasn't taking any chances. I looked down to see where I was and my eyes fell on these words, **"For precept must be upon precept, precept upon precept; line upon line, line upon line; here a little, and there a little."** I said, *"Huh? What?"* I have never read anything like that before. This had to be one of the lesser verses from the Word of God (I thought). I was about to see where in the Bible it was located. Just before I could do that, I had these thoughts run through my mind. *"If I read the next verse, I'll understand that one better."* I don't know if that was my own reasoning, my spirit, or the Holy Ghost whispering to me; I can't say. Well, I looked down and began to read the next text. **"For with stammering lips and an-**

other tongue will He speak to this people." As I was getting to the end of that verse, I felt a release of power from within me like overfilling a water balloon. It felt like I was being filled up to overflowing; but, the lid was still on. I felt a type of pressure from God's power flowing all through my chest.

I sat there in that chair and hardly took a breath. I didn't move. I didn't even look to see where those scripture verses were located. (Don't worry about them if you don't know where they're located. I'm coming back to them very soon. I'm holding out because that was a part of my experience.) As I looked up, I saw the guest speaker was back up at the front. Then he gave an altar call for anyone that wanted the power of God to touch their life. I looked down at my hands. They were starting to feel energized. I thought, *"Lord, I think I can receive from you now. I know you're doing something with me."* I got up and started moving out. The line of people was already halfway back to the doors. As I moved out from my seat and turned into the aisle, I felt that pressure push its way up my throat. When I turned to move into the line, I felt the power go into my jawbone, my gums, my teeth, my tongue, and then into my lips. I stood there and felt almost bug-eyed from the pressure. Now my lips were shaking and trembling. Once again I found myself at that same place of asking God the same question. *"What are you doing to me now, Lord?!"*

When my turn for prayer came, I stood in front of the speaker. I reached my hands up into the air. For a moment he just stood there and looked at me with a grin on his face. Probably thinking, *"We got us a good one here, church."* I think they could tell this was new to me. Just then, he pulled my hands down with my palms facing downward while touching the underside with his fingertips. He said, *"Just relax. Close your eyes. Now, breathe in His presence. Just breathe Him in. Let Him fill you."* So, I did. I shut everything out but his voice and focused on the Lord. At that moment I began to feel hands being laid on my back. This was more of a distraction than a help. *"I'm trying to focus on the Lord's touch instead of yours."* These were the first thoughts that captured my attention. For a moment it pulled my focus away from God. Then my thoughts were, *"Wait till I fall."* I didn't say these things, but; I wanted to. I was trying not to appear rude. It turned out that wasn't going to be necessary. They were moving their hands. So, I started to focus again. My eyes were still closed. I continued to hold out my hands just as I'd done before. I no longer felt the minister's fingertips. I wasn't sure if he was there praying for me or if he had moved on. I opened my eyes and found I was flat on my back looking up towards the ceiling. I was on the floor and didn't even know it! They were not touching me. They were catching me. Wow, what power. I must have been floating. That was the second time I felt a concentration of God's power. It made me dizzy. I think I felt that because there was too much power for my body to handle. That's why I fell back. From that day forth, every time I felt a strong anointing, my lips trembled just like my hands.

CHAPTER 9
WANTING MORE OF GOD

I WANT TO TAKE YOU BACK TO THE BENNY HINN CRUSADE. THE WOMAN WE WERE sitting next to during the Friday meeting was a monthly partner with his ministry. She shared with us what the partner conferences were like. Instead of 15,000 people, there were only around 1,500. Those meetings were smaller and more intimate. There was a close and more personal touch to those services. She said Benny Hinn has even prayed for people one on one there. Sometime later that month I learned that pastor Benny was having a conference in Birmingham Alabama in September. So, wanting more of God, I became a partner and signed up.

From week to week I set out on a quest searching to understand this manifestation the Bible calls our heavenly language. I knew God spoke to me about the baptism of the Holy Ghost. The Word God spoke to me in March proved it. I felt His power in April. I also knew that power manifested several days later. If anyone had a right to walk in it, I did. After all, it's by the baptism of power that the gift of tongues is received. I now had another experience with God's power along with more scripture to back it up. What I couldn't understand was why tongues weren't manifesting. What was holding me back? It was clear this was something God was trying to do. The deeper I went into these ideas, the more limited information seemed to become. Nearly every friend I had at the time never ventured this far into this part of His Word. I kept to myself concerning these things. I searched the scriptures and prayed.

September came around. Waiting for this conference was like waiting for Christmas. I was very excited. This was the first time I'd ever gone away on a long trip alone. It was like a vacation. The first service took place on Wednesday night. There were two on Thursday; a morning session and an evening one, with the same for Friday. There were many different folks around to meet. Everyone had a story to tell. The conference was held at a hotel in downtown. The place was full of people from all over the country. There were even a few there from other countries. On Wednesday evening, while waiting in line, I met a man from a small town in South Georgia. I didn't know it at the time but, this was a divine encounter. He would soon be instrumental concerning something, which was to one day take place.

While I was meeting other people, I sensed something was different. I knew this conference was going to be another turning point. While waiting in line before the service, a woman overheard me talking with my new friend. She seemed interested in my story. I shared a little with her. She responded in amazement. This surprised me. For nothing in my life seemed very interesting before God changed me. She was showing the same type of excitement as my friends from the Bible study class. She looked at me, *"God's hand is on your life. He's going to use you."* Then she asked, *"Are you called to the ministry?"* I said, *"Ah...not yet. Not that I really know of."* I didn't think very much of what she was saying until while seated and talking to someone else. This woman appeared to be studying me. As I watched she leaned over and asked, *"Are you a preacher?"* I said, *"What, me a preacher? Why do you ask?"* She replied, *"Well. I just thought you might be one, that's all."* I began to think, *"Why are all these people asking me if I'm called to preach. Nobody at home has ever asked me questions like these. What are you doing with me now, Lord?"*

Thursday morning, as I waited in line for the doors to open, someone in Pastor Benny's ministry came up to me. They asked if I would be willing to help usher in the services. He showed me what to do. While working, I looked for my friend. Soon I felt a hand on my shoulder. It was a man who worked for the ministry. His name was Kurt. He was Pastor Benny's church coordinator for the crusades. He asked how I was doing and if I enjoyed the conference so far. He asked what my story was and why I was there. After talking for a little while, he took me aside to sit down. I told him more of my story. He sat there hanging on every word. After I was done, he told me, *"I know someone you must meet. His name is Ralph Wilkerson. He has one of the most gifted anointings to help someone receive the baptism of the Holy Ghost with the evidence of speaking with new tongues."* He was working on the book and tape tables. He took me out to meet him.

Mr. Wilkerson was a retired Pastor. I don't know his ministry experiences, but I think he knew Kathryn Kuhlman, simply by the way he referred to her. He was working with a ministry dedicated to keeping her ministry available. He was selling different items like her tapes and videos of her meetings. As we talked, I began sharing recent events only for him to stop me. He said, *"Calm down. Now just relax. You said you know God spoke to you, right?"* I answered back, *"Yes, but..."* He stopped me again and said. *"I don't need to know everything. You know this belongs to you. That's all you need to understand. So, all there is to do now is just receive it. Here is what we need to do. I'm going to lay my hand on your head and begin to pray in English. Then I'll switch to praying in tongues. That's when God will touch you."* Before praying over me, he asked, *"Do you want to know why I know this is going to happen? Because I've seen it happen for hundreds of others over the years in my ministry."* The whole time he was talking I couldn't help but think, *"Yea, right. I'd like to see that myself!"* At that point in my spiritual growth, I thought I didn't know how to believe any more than I was already believing. Nothing I did or experienced seemed to be able to activate the gift of tongues in me up to this point (I thought). Why was this time going to be any different? Maybe you or someone you know has also felt that way. Maybe you have had the same idea. Is this really for real? It is easier to believe for others than for yourself. I don't think I'm the only one who second guesses things.

As he put forth his hand and begin to pray, I noticed nothing was happening. I began to feel as I did back at that church last June. I wasn't sure what might happen if anything. After praying in English, he switched to praying in tongues. I began to pray myself, *"Okay Lord, now what?"* Still nothing seemed to be happening. What do you do in a situation like that? You turn your focus to God and trust His Word. Yes, God will use His servants but, they're not our source; God is. Nobody is where they need to be spiritually. Not one of us has arrived. Keep in mind, God can use anyone to do His work. Never allow men and women to take your focus off God. That also includes focusing on self. Just stand on the Word. Just trust in the Lord. There's no room for second guessing in second chances.

While I thought nothing was going to happen, "It" happened again. I heard God speak to me. He said, **"Through everything, I've brought you here."** (I knew He was referring to the crusade and that church last June.) ***"I've brought Kurt to you so he could bring you to Ralph. What else must I do so that you may believe?"*** It wasn't God's fault I wasn't receiving; it was my own unbelief. The Church is full of folks who choose not to believe. If that's not the case then why do they have so much trouble walking in the things of God? This keeps one from receiving the baptism of the Holy Ghost. The Christian Church is full of people who say God doesn't do that anymore. Don't misunderstand what I'm saying. I'm not condemning those denominations that do not hold to the baptism of the Holy Ghost. I love my spiritual heritage. I didn't want to stay where I was; I wanted to move into deeper and more powerful levels. I guess some believers only hold to what they are told instead of what the Holy Ghost is teaching. This is sad because Jesus is still the baptizer of the Holy Ghost. If someone hasn't experienced that, don't blame God. It's their faith in the Word that has slipped, not God's work or His Spirit!

I knew I had to make a stand. I knew the time was now. I opened my mouth and began to speak as best I could (even if it might have been wrong). At that point, nothing else mattered. God the Father was standing over me waiting for me to take hold of this. He was waiting for me to act. What would you have done? Faith requires action. So, I did the best I could by faith and began to speak in tongues. That man withdrew, sat back in his set and smiled saying, *"You see, I told you God was going to do it."* All of a sudden a serious look came over his face. He sat up, looked at me pointing his finger, *"God's called you to preach… hasn't He?"*

What!? Why did you ask me that? These were the only words I could find at first to respond with. I was blown away at this. Here I was once again at a place where I could hardly turn around without running into God. Talk about catching a guy off-guard. Perhaps, I really knew it was coming and just didn't pay any attention to the other signs. Pastor Ralph just looked at me. I said, *"I was talking to a woman last night.... Then right before the meeting....."* He held up his hand to stop me and responded, *"I know. I sensed something about you as soon as you sat down and we began talking. You see, a few years ago I asked the Lord to bring young men and women that were being called for ministry into my life so I could pray for them. I want to transfer everything God's given me over to His servants before I'm called home. From that day God has been bringing individuals like you across my path."*

That reminds me of 2 Kings 13:21. God's people were going to bury someone, but instead, they cast him into the sepulcher with the prophet Elisha. As they laid his dead body in the grave with the old dry bones of the prophet, this man was raised from death. Though the prophet was dead the power was not. I don't think I'd ever read where Elisha released the anointing God gave him to someone else. It remained there, in that grave in his very bones until John the Baptist was sent. You know you can't take "It" with you. God's power is transferable. Pastor Ralph knew that.

I thanked him for the prayer and went back to my usher's station in the conference room. That morning Pastor Benny preached a message titled, "The four steps of faith: The transfer of the anointing." It was about Elijah's meeting with Elisha and the transfer of the mantle. I tell you what; God's timing can be so close it's scary. At the end of the service, Benny gave an altar call to all who knew they were called into the ministry. As he was finishing the invitation, he called out and said, *"I am only referring to those who know they are called to full-time ministry."* I could hardly believe my ears. This was no less than a deliberate interruption of my life. I remember thinking this couldn't be real. It was too obvious. A part of my soul struggled to grasp it. It was more than I could take in at one time. But, when God reaches out to you like that it's a hard thing to ignore. I will never forget the day when God called me to preach.

> The Church is full of folks who choose not to believe. If that's not the case then why do they have so much trouble walking in the things of God? This keeps one from receiving the baptism of the Holy Ghost.

During lunch Friday I invited my friends up to my room to pray. Afterwards, I overheard my South Georgia friend telling two others about a church he recently visited. In listening, I learned there was a powerful move of God that took place there. He showed them a book that held the account. I'd never heard of the minister or the book, but my interest was captured in only a moment. There were so many things happening that I closed my eyes and began to pray. *"Lord, you have been doing so many things for me over the past two years. Now I see you introducing more. I wonder if you will do something else? Can you bring me that? Will you give me the book?"* The name of the book was called, *The God Chasers*, written by Tommy Tenny.

The conference was powerful. At the end, everyone was prayed for by Pastor Benny Hinn or someone ministering with him. God blessed, healed, delivered, and set people free. I liked it better than the crusades. It was a wonderful experience. I knew I was going back to another conference the next chance I was given.

CHAPTER 10
LORD, SHOW ME YOU'RE GLORY

I DECIDED NOT TO STAY IN ALABAMA FRIDAY NIGHT. I DROVE HOME AND ARRIVED around 3:30 am. I then got some sleep. I awoke a few minutes before 10 in the morning. I was so excited. I felt like a new man. First, there was all that happened in 1997, then God's voice regarding the Baptism of the Holy Ghost, the release of power while at that church last June, my meeting with pastor Ralph, and now I was being called of the Lord to preach. *"Lord, you have brought me a long way."* My thoughts were full and so was my heart. I was different, that's for sure. A little later on that morning, I called the third friend I earlier referred to. I knew he also was called by God and would celebrate with me. He believed in the baptism of the Holy Ghost. I shared with him the events that took place over the past few days. He was more than excited. I think he responded that way because he was looking for God to do something big in his own life. Just then he said, *"That's like this book I've been reading. Do you know who Pastor Tommy Tenny is?"* I asked, *"Who?"* He said, *"Tommy Tenny!"* I responded, *"No, but that name sounds familiar."* He spent the next few minutes telling me about Pastor Tommy. Things like the name of his ministry and where it was located. But, I could not place it. You see, I forgot I asked God to bring me that book. My focus was still on God's call. When he talked about it, he described it differently than my friend from the conference. To him, it was Tommy Tenny this and Tommy Tenny that. The other man described it as, *The God Chasers.* Then after a few moments, he said, *"I can't believe you don't know who Tommy Tenny is!"* I could hear him take a deep breath before releasing a sigh. The tone of his voice was changing. He sounded a little let down because I couldn't relate to it. Then he said, *"Well,* *the name of the book is called, The God Chasers."* The timing was like a key in a lock opening the doors to heaven over me.

In 1 Corinthians 2:9 we read the words, **"But as it is written, Eye hath not seen, nor ear heard, neither have entered into the heart of man, the things which God hath prepared for them that love him."** Sounds like this means we cannot or should not see but certain things. Yes, the Bible says that no one can see God and live. The word also says God raises the dead back to life. I usually observe it being used several times each year. Some of these messages were actually quite profound. I found their focus was not complete for more still remains. The next verse says, **"But God hath revealed them unto us by his Spirit: for the Spirit searches all things, yea, the deep things of God."** Wow! God has revealed them. Not will, but has. Everyone has the right to know who it is they believe in. God wants to have a relationship with His children. We can know Him. We can fellowship with the Spirit. God is real; more real than this world we're living in.

It seemed to me God was doing so many things at one time I could not take them all in. I didn't know how to process it in my mind. I couldn't go around the next corner without running into God! I felt like I was being watched by the Lord at all times. It was as though the Father was searching for every opportunity available to access my life to draw me into His. I wasn't expecting what was about to happen next. There's no way my expectations or imaginations could have seen it coming. At the very mention of the name of that book, the doors of heaven over my life were opened with a discharge of the wind of the Spirit of God. I collapsed as though thrown to the floor! His presence hit me like a train. I saw the glory of God. I saw, in my spirit, the face of Jesus Christ!

If there's one thing in life you sell out for, it's for this! I will never forget what happened to me that day. I was thrown to the floor. I was so overcome with the power of God's presence that my mind shut down on me; I couldn't reason. I couldn't think. It brought me to the very point of being blacked out. As I was coming to, I noticed I was on my hands and knees. My head was drooping downward. I lost much of my strength. I wasn't sure what was taking place. I can remember I was in some sort of silence; because, my hearing was starting to come back. In unison with that, something else took place. I couldn't breathe. My body was also trying to shut down. I was trying to cry but was without the ability to make a sound. I didn't know what had happened. I tried to shake it off. I couldn't. It felt like a muscle cramp, but all over my body. I slowly opened my eyes. I was trying to hold the phone. Though I was very weak, I had enough strength to lift it. I was amazed that something like a phone could be so difficult to hold. I could barely hear my friend's voice. He was calling to me, *"Marty, what's wrong? What happened? Are you okay? Talk to me!"* I could hardly focus enough to even think about what I just heard, much less answer back. When I tried to speak it was no use. I couldn't talk. After a moment I realized I had to say something. I took in the deepest breath I could manage and forced the air out saying faintly, *"I....can't....talk."* At that point, I broke down weeping.

I don't know how long I was on the floor. As I was able to push myself up, I found he still was waiting for me on the other end of the line. I can't remember all he asked or what was said. I do remember one thing. He said, *"Wow, man I've got to give you this book."* I think when the vision hit me I cried out with a loud voice in a shriek. There's no telling what he thought when he heard that. I can't remember asking him about it. Unfortunately, there was nobody there with me at the time. I would have loved being able to hear first hand from an eyewitness account of what my reaction was like. This is my account of what took place physically the day I saw the Glory of God.

Here is what happened with my soul. As I was coming to, I noticed one reason to why I was hit so hard. I saw a vision. For years I've studied the vision. It has only been perhaps one year or so (from the start of writing this book) since I really understood it. I'm sure with the years to come I may understand more. I was on my knees in the vision sitting back on the heels of my feet. My back was arched with my arms reaching up into the air. I was clinching both hands into a fist. My neck was bent so my head could look straight up. I was covered by a shaft of blinding white light that shone down from heaven. It was like being under a stage spotlight. This light was full of the knowledge of the glory of God. It was so bright I seemed to be surrounded by darkness. I found out the darkness that I thought was surrounding me wasn't darkness at all. I came to realize I was under the shadow of the Almighty! The echoes of my cries were still resounding in my mind as I was coming to. *"Oh, the mercy and the faithfulness!"* Those were the words I shouted in the vision as tears streamed down my face. Over the next few days as I read the book *The*

God Chasers, I came to the place in the book which identified this was something Moses saw when God answered his prayer back in Exodus 33:18. Moses asked, **"I beseech thee, shew me thy glory."** God was covering me with His hand as He was passing over me there in my den. The most amazing part was I did not know what was in the book. I never tried to use my faith to make anything happen. It just happened. This was something He chose to do. He was taking me at the very words I spoke while I was at the conference. I did ask the Lord, *"Can you bring me that? Will you give me the book?"* Not only did God bring me the book; but, He gave me that experience.

This is what happened to me in the spirit man. Over the next few days, I began to see an image coming from my spirit to my heart and mind. It was the face of a man. The face was that of Christ Jesus. His face kept appearing to me like a watermark found on a dollar bill. I could see it faintly while in prayer, in worship, and even sometimes throughout the day. It depended on whether or not my thoughts were upon Him. The more I prayed, the more I could see and remember. Soon I realized exactly what took place. The instant I heard the name of the book I realized God had just answered another prayer. For only a flicker of a moment, I knew I was being overtaken and knew it was the Lord that was doing it. I was enveloped by His gaze like being swept under a tidal wave. His face struck like lightning through my spirit man burning its image into me. It was only a flash. Just as the flash of a bright light can burn the silhouette of its image into your eyes, His image was burned in the eyes of my soul and spirit. That reminds of the story where Isaiah was given the live coal (Isaiah 6:6). I then saw my sin. I saw things like pride, greed, doubt, and unforgiveness. I also saw my fears. I felt horrible. I was ashamed. I wanted to go somewhere and hide (if you remember, that's what Adam and Eve did). But, there was nowhere to go to escape Him.

What happened next was the very thing that broke me. This next part is a little more difficult to explain. First, He gave me an understanding of my sin from His point of view. This gave me the ability to understand Him better as He really is. He was giving me something to compare Him to. Secondly, seeing my sin gave me the ability to see how pure He is. It was like His gaze was taking hold of me. Now I could relate to what I was seeing better. I tried to pull away; but, I couldn't move. I was gripped by fear. It was the fear of God. The encounter stunned me too deep to pull away. This fear was the side effect of my sin. Though I felt fear I knew He wanted me to look at Him. He wanted me to know Him. Furthermore, He wanted me to know that He knew me just as I was. When He took hold of me, He made me look. That's when I saw it. I saw how He really felt. I saw the real Jesus. Not the one handed down through Church. I saw God's forgiveness. I saw His mercy, His faithfulness, and His love. He looked at me that day as if I had never known sin before. It was like I'd only known Him. It was like my feet had never touched the ground. At the time my heart was shouting, *"How could you?! How can you?!!"* I found I was thinking this over and over as I collapsed. I saw, felt, and was embraced by His love, mercy, and faithfulness that day. His greatness became intimate to me. A part of what I called life was consumed by the knowledge of His glory. I didn't see heaven that day, but Jesus; He's for real. If only I could find words that have the power to hold a description of Him like the way His presence held me. Can you imagine having the ability to understand something that cannot be comprehended? I began to understand the words of the Apostle Paul a little more as these words resounded within me, *"Oh, that I may know Him and the power of His resurrection."* (Philippians 3:10)

> I began to see an image coming from my spirit to my heart and mind. It was the face of a man. The face was that of Christ Jesus. His face kept appearing to me like a watermark found on a dollar bill.

For God, who commanded the light to shine out of darkness, hath shined in our hearts, to give the light of the knowledge of the glory of God in the face of Jesus Christ - 2 Corinthians 4:6

CHAPTER 11
A NEW LIFE WITH NEW POWER

A sense of heavy caution

THE NEXT DAY WAS SUNDAY. THAT WAS THE MORNING MY CHURCH WAS HAVING their deacon dedication ceremony. I was voted in. The leadership was to lay hands on us. We were being set apart for service. But, having so many experiences with God begin to alter my view point about that church. Up to this time no one there knew how God was leading me. I told no one about the changes. This Sunday morning was my turn to give the offertory prayer. Though I wasn't preaching I felt, in my own small way, this was my time to minister. I stood before the congregation paused for a moment with eyes closed. The church waited silently. All of a sudden the Spirit of God surged through my body. I felt dizzy. It was like having a drug pumped into my blood stream. I began to sway slightly. I immediately opened my eyes. If I had not recovered my balance I would've fell under the power again right in front of everyone!

After the church service, I walked downstairs to leave. It had become my custom to park behind the church. I didn't know it at the time but, I was being followed. This person had only attended the church for a few months. As he came out, I heard the door close behind him. I felt nothing unusual and thought nothing about this until he called out to me. *"Hey, Marty, come here. I've got to talk to you."* I was almost overcome with a sense of heavy caution. I never felt this before. I don't really know how to describe the feeling. The only way I can explain it is to say I felt a form of darkness. It was like my spirit man seemed too divided from my soul as to turn around to look at him! In this, I now knew who it was, though I didn't know how it happened. I wish I could explain it better. I looked within myself saying, *"You see something, don't you Lord?"* No answer was returned to me. It was like my spirit went into a 3D mode. I felt like I had Holy Ghost radar!

I know now that seeing God's glory had activated a part of the supply of the spirit of Christ, which wasn't awakened before. In turning to respond to him, he said, *"I know your family has been very involved in this church for a very long time; but, I think it would be best if you told everyone that you can't be a deacon. You see, the Bible says a deacon is a man of one wife and you don't have a wife."* At hearing those words, I could now reason out what I must have felt in my spirit. That man had a religious demon ministering to him. His response to what I said next revealed that. *"Oh, that won't matter. I don't believe I'll be a deacon long because God's just called me to preach."* All of a sudden that man arched his back and rolled his shoulders in contempt against me. He looked me in the eyes and said with full confidence, *"NO! NO! You can't do that! If you do that the blessings of God won't come on your life!"* I sensed at that moment a spirit was lingering over his left shoulder ministering to him. I could all but see "it" with my physical eyes. I turned and walked away. I called the pastor that afternoon and disused the event. That night he preached on the life of the Apostle Paul and how he wasn't married either. Before long that man was bringing division in the church, and the pastor was forced to ask him to leave. This experience was a learning point for me. As soon as God launches you in a new direction the devil will always show up and try to block or detour you if he can.

> All of a sudden the Spirit of God surged through my body. I felt dizzy. It was like having a drug pumped into my blood stream. I began to sway slightly. I immediately opened my eyes. If I had not recovered my balance I would've fell under the power again right in front of everyone!

Something startling

Over the next few days, I decided to re-examine what the Word taught about speaking in tongues. To tell you the truth, I felt I didn't understand the gift. What if there was more to it. What if nothing really happened? What if I was wrong? I've heard from many individuals that they heard something when the gift of tongues came upon them. I mean they heard what to say. I heard God's voice, not another language. I'd also been told the Holy Ghost may take over at the point of speaking in tongues. Some would even wake up on the floor speaking in their new language. I know God spoke to me about the power and that's for sure. And, I know He spoke to me about tongues as well. But, as far as hearing what I was to say, that wasn't happening. I believed I was baptized in the Holy Ghost, but I didn't receive tongues at that time. That was another point of confusion for me. I know some Christian circles teach if you don't pray in tongues when it happens then you aren't baptized by the Holy Ghost. There are also churches that teach all you have to do is speak (in what sounds like tongues) for the gift to manifest. I have heard others say if you're not baptized in the Holy Ghost that you can't even go to heaven. But, I knew that statement wasn't biblical. I know what the Word says. I also know the baptism of the Holy Ghost is not a baptism of tongues. It is a baptism of Power! The power releases the gifts. Not the other way around. I was allowing my mind and what people from church taught to confuse me.

> I also know the baptism of the Holy Ghost is not a baptism of tongues. It is a baptism of Power! The power releases the gifts. Not the other way around.

I knew I was baptized by the Holy Ghost. I knew what God had done. His power showing up in me has shown me that. I just didn't understand the aspect of our heavenly language.

As I looked in 1 Corinthians 14, I saw something startling. In verse 21, we read, **"In the law it is written, with men of other tongues and other lips will I speak unto this people..."** This verse read like the one God gave me when I was back at that new modern style church last June. Yet, I knew I wasn't in the New Testament, I was reading from the Old. As I looked it up to see what Paul was quoting I saw it was the same verse. Paul was quoting from Isaiah 28:11. God began giving me the gift of speaking with new tongues back at that church, and I didn't even know it. This floored me. My thoughts were, *"You mean I've been beating myself over the head this whole time for no reason!"* I had no idea the Old Testament had anything in it which dealt with speaking in tongues. It turned out I had the release of the gift of tongues. I had it since that service but just wasn't yielding to it properly. It was lying dormant until I chose to activate it. If you have the baptism of power but haven't spoken in tongues, don't worry, just keep pushing in. If it doesn't come after a while, then you just may have to consider that you were never baptized by the Spirit in the first place.

God's hands on your life

A month or so passed. I soon received a call from one of my friends. He invited me to visit his church. He's the one that gave me the book *The God Chasers*. He was going to a Church of God at the time. They were having a special service in a few days. The man scheduled to preach was said to be a prophet. Upon arriving, I wasn't expecting very much. I thought it would be hard for anyone or anything to top what just happened to me. What the man preached was fairly average. Afterwards he gave an altar call. I can't say I saw anything above unusual about that service. I went forward anyway. He laid hands on everyone that came forward. He wanted to see if God would show him anything. After doing so he asked for everyone to go back to their seat. He looked around the room to a few people. He told them to take out a pen and paper. This gave each person a chance to write down every word God gave him to speak over them. When he got nearer to the end he looked over at me. *"Young man, God's hand is on your life. He's about to use you."* Immediately my mind went back to the conference and the words spoken over me; they were the same. I couldn't help but think this meant something; something big. I could see God was speaking to me. There's no way that man could've known anything about what had taken place. Only God could have shown him. So, I held those words close to my heart. I wondered what was coming next.

> If you have the baptism of power but haven't spoken in tongues, don't worry, just keep pushing in. If it doesn't come after a while, then you just may have to consider that you were never baptized by the Spirit in the first place.

Very soon my home church held their fall revival services. In one of these services, I noticed an advertisement for a revival at a different church. This seemed odd as this was not a Baptist church; it was a Spirit-filled one. The church was a one hour drive away. I went up to someone I met during those meetings to show them what I found. He wasn't a member of our church. He was there visiting because of the revival. I thought he might not mind going there with me. He just looked at me and slowly smiled saying, *"I put that back there."* I'm not sure if anyone else noticed it. I think God arranged it that way. This turned out to be another divine appointment. That church was and is to this day a strong, charismatic trans-denominational Christian church. The pastor of that church started it in the early 1970's. He held that position for over forty years before retiring. He was with the Church of God before that. I soon found out, after meeting him, that he was once a pastor from my hometown.

It only took one service for me to see this was where God wanted me to be. As soon as I was able to join that church I did. The very next Sunday morning (from the day I joined) I received confirmation from God on an even deeper level. The pastor announced the church was having a licensing and ordination service that night. He asked if anyone was missed they should come forward after church to let them know. I had a chance to meet with them and share some of what God was doing. They licensed me alone with the others that night. I could hardly believe it. I know they had to take a step of faith to do that; but, it only shows God's hand really was on my life.

A few weeks later, I was sitting on one of the front rows during a Sunday morning service. We had a guest speaker. He was a short,stout man. As he preached he would move back and forth. Rarely did he stay on the platform behind the podium. Then all of a sudden, he stopped in the middle of the service, looked over at me pointing his finger saying, *"God's hands are on your life. He's gonna use you."* Then he went back to his sermon like nothing ever happened. After church, a new friend came up and said, *"Man, you haven't been here for very long and God's already calling you out."* I looked at him and said, *"Wait one minute. You mean to tell me that actually happened. I'm not dreaming. He said that."* To tell you the truth, it was done in such a way I almost wasn't sure if it did happen until I knew others saw it as well. This was the third time in only a few weeks where different ministers from different locations, whom I didn't know and didn't know me, said the same word from God. The same thing happened when God was calling me to preach. He spoke through separate people three different times. Even my experiences regarding the baptism of the Holy Ghost came in three waves. Before God will do anything in your life, He may use others around you to help confirm it. Sometimes, people will see what God is doing in your life before you do. If there's no one around confirming the work of God for your life, then God's timing may not have come for you yet.

More power than before

Soon, I noticed Benny Hinn was having another conference coming up in the spring. As time drew nearer, I was called of God into a 21 day fast. I wasn't sure what God was planning or what He might want to do. There was really no telling what might happen. I expected anything. The conference took place in Tennessee. Upon arriving, I ran into Kurt. He was the one who introduced me to Pastor Ralph. He actually remembered the encounter and took me on back so I could get started working. Though the hours were long, each day was a delight. I enjoyed being involved. It was a labor of love. I soon found out that pastor Benny would be laying hands on everyone at the end of the conference. When the time came, we who served were last in line. When my time came, I felt the power of God unlike any time before. After the service was over, I was talking with the lady that stood next to me. She said God hit me so hard that my arm hit her head and knocked off her glasses. Thank God they weren't broken.

> Then all of a sudden, he stopped in the middle of the service, looked over at me pointing his finger saying, *"God's hands are on your life. He's gonna use you."* Then he went back to his sermon like nothing ever happened.

That was only the first impartation of three that took place. Before I knew it, I was being picked up. I was dizzy. I stood there for only a few seconds before being pushed forward toward the stage. I sort of woke up enough to look ahead. I knew the stage was short and I didn't want to hit my shins. Then I thought, perhaps, I was in the way. As I looked up to see where the stage was, I saw Benny Hinn coming at me with both hands outstretched. That woman told me when I went down that first time Pastor Benny kept looking back at me. She then said, after a minute or two he called out to the catchers, *"Pick that young man up again."*

I never felt the power of God like that before. I know you may not believe me when I say that I could actually see the power (like in a vision)! But, it's true. I could see it. Just before he touched me, I saw something I can only describe as a transparent mass the size of a beach ball. Do you know how the air over a source of heat looks? That's what I saw. It was clear, yet I saw a blurred object as a mass of power appearing above me floating in the air. It was poured into my spirit as though being forced down my throat. It took my breath away. I went down for the second time.

After a few moments they picked me up again. I was standing there in a daze. I thought I could hear the sounds of voices faintly in the background. Shortly, the sounds dwindled down to light chuckles. They were laughing at me. Only I didn't know that at the time. All I could do was stand there. I knew my friend Kurt was beside me. He was gently nudging my arm. I was so drunk in the spirit I couldn't respond to him. I just stood there looking at the floor in front of the stage. Then I felt him nudge me again. I could not respond. I knew he was trying to get my attention, but; it was no use. He bumped me again. This caused me to tilt to one side. I began to shake off this tipsy sensation as I looked up at him. He just smiled. Then he turned his eyes towards the front as though to look at the stage. He was doing this to point me in that direction. I couldn't respond; I was too drunk on the power of the Spirit of God. That's when he looked again and started to point toward the front. He was even talking to me as he did it but, for some reason, I couldn't hear him. Just then the look on his face changed like he was mad at me. He curled his lips, squished his eyes a little, and pointed in front of us and stared at me. That's when the message got through to me. I turned and looked in front of me and there he was. Pastor Benny had been standing there the whole time with arms crossed just looking at me. My mouth dropped open in shock. Then laughter broke forth in the crowd. Pastor Benny then began to ask me a similar question as I've heard from God three times before. *"Are you ready for God to use you young man."* Wow, for some reason I heard him. I said, *"Yea!"* He then said, *"Well, lift your hands and get it."* I closed my eyes and put my focus on God. I took a half step toward the stage. I got my hands part of the way up and saw that power again. It was the size of a small car and it was being shoved down my throat. Pastor Benny didn't have the chance to touch me. I was going down.

My last conference

I think now might be a good time to share my experiences with the next Benny Hinn conference I attended. It took place in Virginia Beach, Virginia. This not only was the third one but the last of them. This situation wasn't about power. It was concerning the most important lesson of all: a lesson on humility. At that time I was feeling a strong drive from the call of God. The Lord put so much power in me but I was without an opportunity to let Him use it. All I wanted to do was serve in some form of ministry. I think each encounter put in my mind the idea that now was the time. What God was about to teach me was to wait for His timing. It's very important to stay on the path the Lord is setting before us. However, it's more important to stay focused on the one who sets your course. But, you must know that I had something on my mind.

If you look at Acts 19:12 you'll find an account where Paul prayed over handkerchiefs and aprons. God anointed those items, so when they went back to their owners, they were healed. Due to God using those first few verses from Acts 19 to speak to me about the baptism of the Holy Ghost, I thought about buying a little bottle of anointing oil to see if Pastor Benny would pray over it. After all, it was Benny Hinn God chose to use for that impartation. If a handkerchief could hold the anointing, then why wouldn't the Holy oil? How perfect for me I thought. Whenever I preached my testimony concerning God's power I could anoint people with that oil when I prayed. Now, for all of you religious folks out there, I knew Benny Hinn wasn't the source of God's power. I also understood that oil was just oil. I only did this because God chose to use him alone with those verses.

When I arrived at this conference I didn't come across anyone I knew from before. I had to ask around. I was finally admitted in after a little difficulty. In doing so, I found that many of the ushers were already placed into position. I looked around. The same man I met during my first conference, the one from South Georgia, was now a staff volunteer. It was he who was in charge of the ushers for those services. I thought to myself, *"I'll get a good place to work at this conference."* One by one he placed them all out until there were only five of us. That's when I knew something was not quite right. He took the remaining ushers back with him and placed them where they needed to be. Then turned towards the main doors and was gone. I was left alone sitting on the platform.

I realized right off that he wasn't coming back. This bothered me. I was afraid this might happen. The idea had been going through my mind for days. In addition to that, I had some trouble getting there. I felt some sort of resistance against me. The way things went up to this point made me feel moody. For some reason, I was afraid they might not need me. I didn't like it at all. Think back to my first turning point. The mood I was now carrying is just like that one. Do you know what that indicates? I was at another turning point. While sitting on the stage, I told God, *"If I can't serve, I should have stayed at home. I came here to be used. Is that not your will for me, Lord?"* The Lord then spoke audibly to me in these words, ***"Do you remember when I found you?"*** He was referring to the conference where I was asked to help usher. Then He said, ***"When I want to use you I will come and get you myself."*** This humbled me. I dropped my head in repentance. I went out to find my friend. I let him know if he needed me for anything he only had to ask. He looked at me in surprise. *"What? I do need you. Didn't I give you a place?"* I said, *"No."* He took me to the back of the conference room. *"I'm sorry but everywhere else is taken. Will it be okay if I put you back here to work"?* I told him it was fine. I was happy to have it. I was happy just to serve.

The next day I ran into my friend Kurt. I showed him that bottle of oil. He looked at it then looked at me. He opened the small bottle, smelled it to see if it was real. He looked up while grinning and said, *"I'll take care of it for you."* Later on, I ran into him and asked if he saw Benny. He said, *"Yes, I did, and I told him about you. Pastor Benny said that he doesn't like having things in his pocket while he's preaching."* Then he looked at me with much excitement and said, *"But, he did tell me to bring him the oil just before he prays for all the people Friday night. He said he would take it then."* He smiled and nodded his head at me as he turned to walk away.

The people that sat in the back arrived late and left early. I got the impression from some they were only going along for the ride. Their attitude didn't reflect the look of passion and expectancy. That didn't matter to me. I was determined to enjoy the services. Before each meeting, I walked around and talked to almost everyone who sat back there. I asked them questions like, *"What's God doing in your life?"* On Friday morning I had a visitor from the front. He worked in Benny Hinn's ministry for years. Charlie was over the alter workers. He said he'd been watching me. *"Marty, I've been observing you the entire conference. I'm going to need some help up front tonight when Pastor Benny prays for everyone. I want you to help me."* This caught me off-guard, to say the least. I didn't see that coming. This was something I was waiting for since the conference began. Just like that, I was being moved to the front.

Ever since God called me I've had a drive that made me want to be close to the action. I wanted to be involved. Soon I realized God did this on purpose to get my attention. I could almost hear the Lord say, *"I told you I would come to get you."*

Just then another man approached me. He said, *"I've been watching you. I need some help with the wheelchairs tonight."* I said, *"Charlie just asked me to help him."* Then he said, *"Don't worry about Charlie. I'll talk to him later."* As not to have any confusion, I immediately went down front to find Charlie. Soon the two men were almost fighting over me. It was somewhat humorous. All of a sudden Charlie, while waving his hand up and down in front of me, said, *"I need him. I can't just put anybody in front of Pastor Hinn. I'll find you someone else."* They trained me to catch and work the alter. I was right in the middle of what was going on. I was in the thick of things. I worked with those who worked right next to Benny. I'll never forget those services. It was a wonderful experience being so close to what was taking place and meeting people that worked in a ministry like that.

I have one more thing to share about the last conference. It was the ushers' job to help clean up and break down the stage. Just as I was doing so, I heard a voice call my name. It was Kurt. I forgot all about the bottle of oil. He waved me over to him. As I came up, he stretched out his fist. He had something in his hand. It was the oil. He slipped it to me quietly, smiled and turned away saying, *"Use it well."*

I had to learn a similar lesson in my new church home. It was during a weeklong conference held there. I was feeling that same edgy push in my soul to serve. As each day went by a sense of anger was growing within me. This feeling was from the sin of covetousness. Once again I desired to be close to the action. Toward the end of the week a friend asked if I could take him home after the meeting. After it was over, I couldn't find him. In asking around I was told, *"Oh, he's upstairs with the ministers eating."* He wasn't one of the pastors. This was no less than another test. It was a slap in the face is what it was. I had to wait for him until he was ready to go. That left me feeling more anger. The next night, which was the last, I can remember standing around killing time before going. I didn't want to leave. I wanted to be upstairs with the ministers. I knew I was wrong in my heart. So, I decided to leave. I sat in my car for a moment. However, I knew I had to go sooner or later. It was almost 10 pm and I still had an hour to drive in order to get home. I can remember taking a deep breath and sighing. It was almost like letting go was breaking my heart a little. I guess this sounds a little silly to you. The way I felt then was the same as I did back at my first turning point. I started my car, but I just sat there. I guess I hoped something might happen. Well, something did happen. While backing out, I looked up to see the pastor's granddaughter running on the sidewalk. I turned and looked to each side to see where she was going. There was no one left in that part of the parking lot. I looked to see if I'd left my Bible. No, it was beside me. *"Marty, I've been looking for you everywhere. They want you to come upstairs to eat with them."* As soon as you let go, you are giving God room to take hold. If there is something in your heart you really want, let the Lord give it to you. God wants to bless you.

CHAPTER 12
HUMILITY IS THE KEY

THE EXPERIENCE GAINED FROM MY LAST CONFERENCE REMINDS ME OF A PASSAGE of scripture found in Luke 14:8-11. It's a story about someone being invited to a gathering like a wedding. In this passage, Jesus teaches that we should not try to seat ourselves in an important place (the KJV referred to seat as room). He emphasized it would be more notable for us to take the lower place. When I humbled myself before God, He opened the door of advancement for me. The Word of God is full of truth that describes how vital it is to have humility at work in our life. Sometimes the encounter we have with Him is going to be more important than the type of work we've been called to do. Knowing Him comes first. Furthermore, how does anyone expect to do the work of God if they don't know how to first be a servant? Being humble is the key. Not following it can, and will almost certainly, one day give birth to pride in our life. It doesn't matter how much power you walk in if your heart isn't right with the Lord. God will always respond to our humility long before He will ever respond to our qualifications.

Over the past few years, I've come to see how closely love and humility work together. The Apostle Paul said in 1 Corinthians chapter 13:1-3, "Though I may be able to speak with the tongues of men and angels, have the gift of prophecy, understand all knowledge and mysteries, have all the faith of God, feed the poor, and even die for the cause of Christ but have not charity, I have nothing." What's the use in gaining power if that's all you seek after? That's what the devil wants, and that's the reason Adam and Eve lost position in the Garden of Eden. It doesn't matter how much authority you have access to if your character isn't developed enough to keep it. Think about this, you wouldn't give a child or teenager a loaded gun if they couldn't be responsible with it? Christ Jesus said in Matthew 7:22-23, **"Many will say to me in that day, Lord, Lord, have we not prophesied in thy name? And in thy name have cast out devils? And in thy name done many wonderful works? And then I will profess unto them, I never knew you: depart from me, ye that work iniquity."** To seek after God's power without desiring His heart may lead us to the highest level of sin.

Not one thing in that list dealt with the labor of love. If we want to walk upright before God, we must walk in love while doing His work. Yes, we need God's power; but, we can't sacrifice the love walk for it! What if the love walk is the key to finding the power? What if humility is the key to walking in love more effectively? I have seen God use many ministers to do mighty things. But, their reward won't be based on how much power they access. The Bible teaches us that works without faith is dead. So also, labor without love is dead. What if we miss His purpose because we're focused on the power instead of focusing on His love, which is the source of His power? Christ Jesus said in Mark 9:35, **"If any man desire to be first, the same shall be last of all, and servant of all."** Christ Jesus said, by doing this, we would be the greatest in the kingdom of Heaven. Therefore, in every work of God you do, do it all through the focus of the labor of love. What if the only record of reward we retain in heaven is from our labor of love here on earth?

"Remembering without ceasing your work of faith, and labor of love, and patience of hope in our Lord Jesus Christ, in the sight of God and our Father." – 1 Thessalonians 1:3

CHAPTER 13
THE SPIRIT OF THE SUPPLY OF CHRIST

THE EVENT I'M ABOUT TO MENTION TOOK PLACE AROUND LATE SUMMER IN THE year 2000. I stopped by my parent's house to see how things were going. Mom was at home, but dad was working. It was Saturday. She was doing some work on the computer. I noticed a pack of CD's sitting on the monitor. *"Mom, what's this?"* It was a three-CD set of Mozart's Greatest Hits. For years I'd been listening to Classical music. I started back in my college days. It developed into a small passion. I use to listen to heavy metal and other types of rock music back in my old days. I switched to classical in my early 20's. Classical music was now a part of who I was.

"When did you buy this? Can I borrow them?" I asked. She looked up replying, *"Oh. You'll have to ask your brother about them. They'....that's his."* He was still living at home. (This is not the same person I earlier referred to. This is my other brother.) I wasn't expecting them to belong to him. Some of the music he listened to at the time was known as shock rock. The main one was Marilyn Manson. For those of you who don't know him; that was some seriously bad stuff. This was just after he released his album "The Anti-Christ Superstar." My Sunday school teacher from the Baptist church did a little research and said he found out if you followed the guidelines on Manson's internet web site, you could get *"born again in his name through his satanic church."* Then Manson would send you a hand signed birth certificate with your name on it. In other words, you could get born again in his name instead of the name of Jesus.

THE WORK OF GOD   93

I know there have always been unconfirmed rumors about people like Manson and Ozzy Osbourne. Yet, there's one thing I know to be true. I heard Manson say in a TV interview that he feels he has always identified with *"the character of Lucifer from the Bible."* Why would anyone want to pattern their life after Lucifer? How can someone of a logical mind say things like that? This was the mess my brother was getting into. This was some really bad stuff! They were seeds of the devil in the lives of that generation. It's sad to see people like Manson take satanic or worldly influence to the degree they have. The devil must have known the potential they would've had. He must have seen what kind of visionaries they would be one day and knew the negative change that would be inflicted on the world. It's too bad they served Satan and self instead of Jesus. It's too bad they didn't want to live for Christ and the work of God.

"I know who you are. You may be using a different man with him than you used over me but, you are that same spirit. I broke your power over my life and now..... I break your power in and over his. In Jesus name!"

(Oh, and as for Ozzy; I know he claims to have joined to the Church of England. Yet, joining a church won't save you. Giving huge sums of money to church won't either.) If he is now a real Christian, he should try recalling every music work from his past instead of continuing to sell and make money off them. The Word of God says to not give the appearance of evil. After all, who is he trying to represent now, God or the devil and this world? Death and darkness or light and life? The bottom line is, there are many which may talk the talk but can they walk the walk? I know he can't go back in time to prevent the music from ever being made. Yes, God can forgive our past. He forgave mine. However, if I had published writings on bookstore shelves which taught against the Word of God, I would now want to do everything within my power to recall as many of them as I could and no longer allow more of them to be put into print.

A few months earlier my brother was growing into a place in his life where he felt he was growing out of his faith in God. I'm sure that music, and others like it, had something to do with it. While Mom and I were talking about the Lord with him, he shared his unbelief. Mom said, *"We saw you go to the altar and get saved. You were also baptized. So, are you telling us that meant nothing?"* I don't think she was ready to hear what he had to say back. He replied, *"I only did that because y'all would never leave me alone. I never believed."* Then he walked away.

Not long after this took place some friends from my new church home were going to another church out of town to attend a Kenneth E. Hagin meeting. I heard of him from that church I visited in June. I only mention this because, while I was at Kenneth's meeting, I was able to get a prayer cloth like the ones you read about in chapter 19 of the book of Acts. I was planning on slipping the cloth between the two mattresses in my brother's bed. Later that week, I got my chance. He wasn't home. When I walked in his room the air was different. It felt eerie and somewhat thick or heavy. Not at all like my prayer room, which was light and fresh. It was just the opposite. I looked around to see several Anti-Christ Superstar posters on his wall. I pulled out the bottle of anointing oil and began to pray over and anoint the cloth. I knew I had the right and the power to stop that unclean spirit. At one time in my life, I dealt with and broke the power of that type of spiritual influence over my own life! This influence came to me through Ozzy. I pointed my finger at those images, looking pass the picture on the paper, and said, *"I know who you are. You may be using a different man with him than you used over me but, you are that same spirit. I broke your power over my life and now..... I break your power in and over his. In Jesus name!"* I laid my hands on those posters and rebuked them in the name of the Lord. Then, I slipped the cloth under the top mattress. Turned and walked out closing the door behind me.

This now brings me up to the time when I knocked on his bedroom door to ask for the CD's. In opening the door, I noticed the posters were gone. I asked him if I could borrow the Mozart CD's. I then looked around to see not one picture remained. *"Hey, didn't you have some rock music posters hanging on your walls? What happened to them?"* He answered saying, *"Oh....I got tired of them. So....I took them down."* I was perplexed to say the truth about it. It was puzzling. Who goes from Marilyn Manson to Mozart? All the way home I thought it over. Then I began to realize something. It wasn't Kenneth Hagin who was transferred. It wasn't Benny Hinn either; it was something in me. My love for classical music was showing up as an influence in him. I guess having grown in the power of Christ to break the control of that type of spirit gave me the freedom to break it over others. I know it's the Lord in us that's doing the work. We in and of ourselves are no better than anyone else if we don't have

> Having grown in the power of Christ to break the control of that type of spirit gave me the freedom to break it over others. I know it's the Lord in us that's doing the work. We in and of ourselves are no better than anyone else if we don't have Christ.

THE WORK OF GOD

Christ. The Apostle Paul said, as a believer, we all have a supply. Philippians 1:19 referred to this as **"the supply of the Spirit of Jesus Christ."** Your spirit is a container of the resources of God you will need for living life! That day I saw the results of the power of Christ breaking the power of the devil! So, what kind of supply do you think you may be carrying?

CHAPTER 14
WHO IS ON THE LORD'S SIDE?

I SOON BEGAN TO WITHDRAW FROM TELEVISION MINISTRY PREACHERS. THE number of years that passed since my encounters with God in 1997 was showing me how effective the Holy Ghost was as a teacher. I was gaining knowledge from Him that surpassed what I saw being presented by most. Only a few like Benny Hinn remained. Not to say that God wasn't using the others in some way or another. In most cases they were no more than motivational speakers, not preachers. I saw psychology instead of the revelation of God's truth. It's the anointing which breaks the yoke of carnal bondage; not one's gifting. I also found the local church could help me in my walk with God more than they could. I'm not saying they were all strange or religious. Nor am I saying all those preachers we have now are. It's only that I was and am still moving into a new place of maturity in Christ. I guess what I'm trying to say is, *"If you're the smartest or most spiritual one in your group, then it's time to find a new group."*

Many years have passed now since God used Benny Hinn and the others I've mentioned. It grieves my heart and spirit to now hear and sometimes see where some of the Church is heading. I never saw anything questionable with Benny Hinn. I think what was being said was just talk or opinion; nothing more than that. What I'm referring to are the others who are out there now. This is not limited to those on TV. This problem is found all over this country in small to large Churches everywhere. Some have watered down the truth to no more than counsel. They give God's Word with very little direction producing no real change. I have also heard and seen their open and unashamed sin. I feel the need to report this. I have to protect my witness of the Lord Jesus Christ regarding my service to God. So, if what I'm about to say offends you, I'm sorry.

I know none of us are perfect and won't be until the day Christ returns. But, some are not teaching the truth. Maybe they don't know what it is they're doing. Perhaps they twist the truth to fit their point of view or just bring it straight out. It doesn't matter. A lie is a lie and a sin is a sin. Now, if you knew a minister was a liar, you wouldn't listen to them preach, would you? Would you trust a thief with the job of receiving the tithe and offering? NO, you wouldn't. Why would someone allow a thief that won't stop stealing to receive the money of the Church? That reminds me of those prosperity teachers who describe God as no more than a cash box. *"Wait now Marty, you shouldn't judge that person."* Really; is that what you think? I understand that many won't attend church because of someone judging them. Yes, there is a line not to cross. However, there is also a standard to live by! Have you never read where the Apostle Paul wrote to the Church in 1 Corinthians 5:12, **"Do not ye judge them that are within?"** *"Well, I know that God can forgive everyone. We all have sinned. Jesus died for sinners. So, they should have as much right to go to heaven as anyone else."* You must understand the Word of God sets the standard for truth, right, and wrong. A person's opinion doesn't. Furthermore, the life they choose to live won't change it. Neither will their religion or how they believe.

I know this may be hard for some people to read. People who feed on religion will always choke on the truth. So don't misunderstand me. I'm not saying that God doesn't love them or you. I know He does. Furthermore, I also know only the Lord can change someone. What I'm discussing with you is this. If the world wants to stay "The world," then let it. But, the Church must be God's Church. I also know we all have sinned and fallen short of the glory of God. I'm not talking about a mistake. Though we all sin, do you live in it daily? Do you want others to accept it as an alternative lifestyle? Are you trying to live your life out of the sin your committing? There is a huge difference between someone repenting and someone not wanting to repent as if they are living a life that's okay before God. If you sin, turn from it. Do not walk in sin daily and expect it to be accepted as though it's not a sin.

Now, if you wouldn't allow a thief to take up the money for the Church, or allow a liar to have the pulpit, then why do so many which call themselves Christians, accept the sin of homosexuality (this includes all forms, such as lesbians and trans-genders) in their church leadership? Why do these people expect everyone to accept them as a homosexual when they don't freely accept some other sin like being judgmental, having pride, or being greedy? If these are sins then why isn't homosexuality a sin? Why is this no longer a sin when the other acts are being called sin? If you won't let a thief take up the money of the Church then why are so many allowing a homosexual serve as a leader or give the Word of God? I'm not saying that we as the Church should run them out. No. We should be there for those who need God's help and deliverance. For many years now sexual sin has been seen in church and in Christian ministries. It's horrible that the Church now has no shame in being open with it. These so-called Christians must stop "that sin" and repent of their wicked ways before they should be allowed to serve in a place of honor. Their place is at the altar of repentance, not behind the pulpit or in the place of a church leader!

Are they trying to remove the truth of repentance from the Church? Why are they doing these things? Most people don't go into church flaunting their sin in a prideful way as though they boast of it. It's almost like many church homosexuals today want everyone to know and see how happy they are with themselves. Christ Jesus said it would be better if these types of people would commit suicide by hanging a millstone around their neck and jumping into the water than to offend the little children (Matthew 18:6). Do you know who the little ones are? They are those who would've been born again if it was not for their sin. They are a bad witness for Christ because they do not represent the image of God. Too many have been hurt because of the sin of the Church. No true Christian church should present any form of worldly corruption. That's not a presentation of Christ Jesus. This is the very problem the Apostle Paul had as mentioned in Romans 1:25-28. According to him, these types of people had to be sick in soul and spirit to do such things. A sin is still a sin, my friends. If they're going to be in the Church, they must stop acting like the world. Sin must be called what it is and homosexuality is just as much a sin as all the rest. Wrong is wrong, it's that simple.

The reason I'm writing this is because of something that has taken place in our country only a few days from me writing this part of the book. As for true Christians, we have now entered into a time of more spiritual darkness for our country. The Supreme Court has passed the rights for same-sex marriage in every state in the United States of America. They have overlooked the heart of God's people for a heart after this world. They will one day stand before God's true justice and answer for what they have done. As for those who stand with them now, they will also have to stand with them then as well. I see the gap between right and wrong closing in. There are nearly no more gray areas remaining. All these places are either falling into darkness or coming to the light. Soon there will be no more shadows left for a carnal Christian to hide in. You will have to choose one side or the other. The middle ground is disappearing. You will follow this world or follow God.

> We are to reject the sin, not the sinner. We must love them as God loves us. We are either standing with the God of the Word or we're standing for the god of this world. We are either walking in the spirit or walking after the flesh. You must take a stand for the truth if you're a child of God.

To accept God's stand for this doesn't mean we are rejecting others; even if it's one of your own family members. We are to reject the sin, not the sinner. We must love them as God loves us. We are either standing with the God of the Word or we're standing for the god of this world. We are either walking in the spirit or walking after the flesh. You must take a stand for the truth if you're a child of God. If you don't, then you're standing with the devil. For the stand you make will either be in the light or in darkness. You can't stay in the Church and live like the world any longer. Now is the time when we will see who the real people of God are or we will see only their religion. The day is coming and now is when we will see who is on the Lord's side.

This is not judgment that is directed at one individual or another. This is a call to those who consider themselves a part of the Church of the living God to wake up from their sleep (1 Peter 5:8). No one will find God if they're looking for the world. Think not that I say what I do because I'm not walking in God's love. I know some who call themselves homosexual. I have gained their respect because I have shown them love. They know I'm no hypocrite. It's possible to stand upright before God and show His way while showing His love along the way. I've done it. I have even been invited to a "gay people church." He was from the Atlanta area. This was the first time he had gone as well. This was his roommate's church. So, I went. I could hardly believe my eyes and ears. They were very good at twisting the Word of God to mean what they believe. After we left, he looked at me with concern and asked what I thought. I simply said, *"It might look sweet and innocent, but this is not a house of God. They have been deceived and are living a lie!"* To my amazement, he said, *"Yes, something about that just doesn't seem right to me either."*

I didn't find God there that day; only this world. I no longer argue about things like that with others. I understand everything of this sort came through Adam's spiritual death. Homosexuality is NOT in God's nature. This emotion or idea is not being supplied to you by the spirit of Christ. It comes through Adams spiritual death. God wants us to be restored from sin, not hold to it. It's our choice. God's nature gives us the power to choose. To accept sin is to embrace the fall of man. To accept Jesus is to embrace the truth. Just because we all came into this world spiritually dead is no excuse to embrace sin. If you've been born again, Jesus has set you free from that.

> God wants us to be restored from sin, not hold to it. It's our choice. God's nature gives us the power to choose. To accept sin is to embrace the fall of man. To accept Jesus is to embrace the truth. Just because we all came into this world spiritually dead is no excuse to embrace sin. If you've been born again, Jesus has set you free from that.

Now, having said that, I can say I know some were born with a nature to steal. Other tendencies may include a desire to kill. There is also a spirit of self-centeredness. There is a spirit of pride and one of greed. You may not be the same as another; we're all a little different. Then there are those who say they were born homosexual. So what! Get born again and change your nature. I did. I know I was born with a sin nature, but I got born again. I chose not to live after this world. I have chosen to surrender my life to God's truth. All of us were born with a sin nature. You don't have to stay that way. That's the whole point of getting born again. God takes away the old nature and gives us the very nature of His only begotten Son, Jesus. This does not ensure you won't struggle with temptation. No one has arrived. We're all in a process of change. God by His Spirit and Word is still at work in us. There's more of Christ for every believer to walk in. Just because someone falls short of God's glory is no excuse for another to live any way they want. All will answer to God for the life they choose to live here on earth.

The truth is it's not God's fault how we were born. Sin came through Adam and Eve, not God. So, stop blaming God for it! The Lord didn't make you the way you are. Sin did. The job of the true Church is to help someone come out of sin. Not to try to find a way to live with it. That's the entire point. We are supposed to be fighting the darkness, not joining it. Unfortunately, the direction some in the Church have taken over the past few years indicate many want to live their way instead of God's. They deny Christ in the act of accepting self. They walk after the flesh and not the spirit man. They are blinded to the truth and accept it openly. I can see it's not getting better, but worse. As I stand back and look at things today, it has become obvious how the wolf is no longer wearing sheep's skin. The wool has been pulled over the eyes of some in the Church. May God forgive them and us!

If a man also lie with man, as he lieth with a woman, both of them have committed an abomination – Leviticus 20:13

CHAPTER 15
GOING TO ANOTHER LEVEL

NOW IT WAS 2002. FOR THE LAST TWO YEARS, I SERVED AND GREW IN CHRIST through the local church. I did ushering, visitation work, some street ministry, visited the jail, nursing home ministry, and fed the hungry on the street. Into my third year, I stopped driving out on most Wednesdays. Working during the week made the trip too long. So, I joined up with that little country church where my friend and her mother attended. This soon opened the door to serve more in ministry. I became friends with one of the ministers in that house of believers. He had the idea to start a campground ministry in one of our local parks. Throughout that year we ministered to a significant number of people. He came across someone that attended one of the meetings. Though 15 years had passed; they still remember how God used us to speak into their life. I continued assisting their church in a little teaching, preaching, and doing most of the campground services. During October, I found out that someone I knew from my Boy Scout troop was an Evangelist and would be coming to do a revival. God was using him mightily. I didn't know it at the time but, this wasn't the only encounter we would have. I didn't see at first how God had plans for me in this.

As the New Year approached, one of my friends asked if I wanted to visit another church with him. *"There's a big revival coming up in your hometown in a few days right up the road from where you live. Do you want to go and check it out one night?"* The services went on for over three weeks. I know that might seem religious to some people; but, that's what we liked. It didn't bother us.

We were not only God chasers; we were revival chasers. (This was one of the reasons I no longer felt the need for TV preachers). Church was not only another way for us to experience God move in our lives, but; it was another opportunity for us to give Him more of ourselves. Our hunger for God was just that strong. My friend used to say things like, *"I partied like I walked with the devil nearly every night back when I was lost. The least I can do at this point is give the time I now have to God."* On one of these nights that Evangelist was preaching. As I sat there, I was picking up on something in my spirit. When I finally heard God speak, it was in the form of a knowing. It was a knowing which was so real it was logical. I saw myself traveling with him in service to God. I knew what God was asking me to do. He wanted me to drive this evangelist to his meetings, and that's just what happened.

He grew up in the same small town as I did. He believed from an early age that he was called into some kind of ministry. It was easy to see God's hand was on his life from the start. I won't go into all of his testimony, but; the devil tried to do everything he could to stop him from following the call on his life.

> *"I partied like I walked with the devil nearly every night back when I was lost. The least I can do at this point is give the time I now have to God."*

One of the most interesting parts of his testimony dealt with the day he was baptized in the Holy Ghost. He was attending a Southern Baptist college at the time. He would say, *"I think they had the idea of grooming me for a very prestigious First Baptist Church in the Atlanta area."* In one of his classes, he was required to do a term paper on what they called "The charismatic cult." They viewed churches which believe in the baptism of the Holy Ghost with the evidence of speaking in other tongues was not of God. They believed that came from the devil. He found a small Pentecostal Christian church that was having revival and slipped in to observe it quietly. Little did he realize that God was going to call him out. When he found himself at the altar, the old preacher man asked what he thought about being baptized in the Holy Ghost. (He didn't believe in the baptism of the Holy Ghost at that time.) The preacher soon asked Him, *"If it's from Jesus, will you take it?"* He replied, *"If it's from Jesus; of course I will. He saved me and set me free from the bondage of sin!"* The old man then quoted verses from the Word of God, which applied to it. Then barely touched his forehead with the very tip of one finger and prayed. All of a sudden the power of the Holy Ghost began to come over him. It started with his feet and went up from there. The power knocked him to the floor. He rolled from one side of the altar to the other praying in the Holy Ghost the whole time. I asked him what his experience was like. *"What did you feel as the power was beginning to come over you?"* He simply replied, *"It was like hot water was moving up my whole body from my feet to my head. Then, all I can remember was waking up on the floor speaking in tongues!"*

Some folks said he had one of the most powerful evangelism ministries in our area. He was a man putting God and His kingdom first. But he was also smart. He not only knew the Word of God and could follow after the ways of the Lord; but, he knew people. He knew how to minister to someone. I witnessed many things during our time together. Everything from different types of healings to deliverances accompanied with multiple salvations. I have also witnessed that man's words not falling to the ground until they performed what it was he sent them to accomplish. I believe him to be a born leader. Success followed him in whatever he tried to do. It didn't matter if he was working a normal job, helping to build up a church, out evangelizing, a church pastor, or organizing some sort of outreach project. He also was trans-denominational. He would be speaking at a Baptist church one week, and the next week; we go to a Pentecostal church. The anointing he carried produced results for God's kingdom. There were a great number of people that respected the work of God in his life. They knew he was being as real as he could where God was concerned. The man was down to earth and a real people person. He held much honor of God in my eyes. As the years have passed, that honor has never left, and I can't see it ever will. I'm not trying to imply he's perfect. All I'm saying is he's real. He's real with people and real with God. That's all anyone should expect. He was, and is to this day, a brother to me in the Lord. I have a deep love for him and his family.

Meeting him was part of God's plan for my life. We were together for nearly seven years. He was an evangelist for the first year then stepped out again into the pastoral. I already ministered in two different denominations, but through his aid and support, there were three more with two trans-denominational ministries. I served under him as a pastoral elder, deacon, children's pastor, singles pastor, altar worker coordinator, evangelist, and of course his driver.

After I was with him ministering felt different than before; there was more power. During the summer of our first year, I was exposed to a level of God's power I never felt before. It came through being his armor bearer. The power was so strong at times I can remember thinking I didn't feel like the same person. This first took place at that same church just up the road from my home. I was invited to speak one Sunday morning. As I ministered to the congregation, they placed a demand upon Christ in me. That demand activated my supply of the spirit of Christ Jesus making the power of God available to the people. I never thought I would see and feel such a powerful anointing. The altar was full. A great many received a touch from God. I've seen God use others mightily. This was the first time I was used this way.

After getting home, I put on something more comfortable. While looking in the mirror, I didn't recognize the face looking back at me. I can't explain it. It was like looking at a new person. I remember thinking to myself, *"Who are you?!"* I really believe, as I preached, Christ in me took over and that was still working on me. Slowly over the next four hours, that special anointing was lifting. I started to feel normal again. Before, I could feel the strength of the Holy Spirit. After a while, I only felt my spirit. I never knew how draining the power of God could be. I was becoming so tired I couldn't stay awake at church that night. I even had to pull over to rest three times before I could make it home safely. Wow, what a power! To God be all the glory!

> That's when I saw a powerful truth. Position places demand upon the anointing, not who we are. That's why power was available to me when I preached. It wasn't about who I was. For me, that was a higher place of spiritual authority than before.

After joining my second home church, I met their evangelist. I looked for an opportunity to ask him questions about the ministry and the power of God. I loved the manor and style of his preaching. His delivery was different than most. I enjoyed listening to him more than I did the associate pastor. I felt a type of freshness in his messages. Maybe I could relate to him more because of his call. I'm not sure. However, there seemed to be more of God's power available for the associate pastor than for him. So, I asked, *"How does it make you feel to not see as many people respond to God under your preaching than under theirs?"* He then said, *"I'm the evangelist. As the associate pastor, they're in a stronger position of authority for this church."* That's when I saw a powerful truth. Position places demand upon the anointing, not who we are. That's why power was available to me when I preached. It wasn't about who I was. For me, that was a higher place of spiritual authority than before. I've learned no one can promote themselves. Just look back to what I said about humility. Not even Jesus exalted Himself. It was John the Baptist who acknowledged Him openly to the people. If you're going to be honored, let God do it. Never exalt yourself. We must be sure people are following the Lord instead of us. If we're not careful, we'll open the door to pride.

The Lord entered through the door God used John to prepare. John 10:3 said he opened the door for the shepherd to enter. Opening the door was a shadow type that meant he revealed the truth found in the Word which was before hidden from them. In that, Jesus was the one the Word was referring to. One thing is certain. The door for your ministry will always be found in another established ministry. We see this repeated again and again. We have been sent into this world to be a witness of Jesus. Christ Jesus came through the ministry of John the Baptist. John the Baptist came under the power of the spirit of Elijah which was given to Elisha. Elisha came by the power of the mantle of Elijah. No one will be qualified to carry an anointing until they first serve. If you don't submit to one, you won't carry one. The Centurion from Matthew 8:5-13 understood this. He was a man carrying authority because he was a man under authority. You will never carry more than you're willing to submit to! The level of your anointing will result from the level of your submission. The deeper you go into submission, the higher God can take you.

> It's amazing what you can sometimes see when the Holy Ghost moves in power. But, it's even more amazing when it's you He chooses to use.

You shall receive power!

It's amazing what you can sometimes see when the Holy Ghost moves in power. But, it's even more amazing when it's you He chooses to use. One of the most memorable teaching events that came through the Spirit of the Lord took place in 2004. The evangelist I was driving was now a pastor. The church began holding Thursday evening prayer services. In one of these services, something took place which marked me. Halfway through I noticed he was praying for several people. I came alongside to aid him. A sense of conviction swept over me. It was a driving, pulling desire to pray for the lady he was ministering to. I didn't think much about it. I just shook it off. Within seconds it returned. Straightway I said to myself, *"What could I possibly release for her that you're not doing through him Lord?"* I got an immediate response. I heard the Lord speak these words, **"I have made you an elder in this church. You need to act like one. Lay your hands on that woman and pray for her."**

As soon as he finished, she turned and looked at me. I said, *"Um.... The Lord also wants me to pray for you."* With a smile, she answered saying, *"Yes, please do."* I wasn't sure what was going to take place. I will admit I knew God believed in me more than I believed in myself. Yet, I obeyed His command. I'm glad I did. As soon as I finished a strange look appeared on her face. I asked, *"What is it?"* She responded, *"I have never experienced anything like that before."* *"Like what?"* I said. *"When the Pastor was praying for me it felt like hot water was moving over my feet and up my legs. As he kept praying, it kept moving up. Then, when he stopped praying, it stopped. What was that?"* I could hardly believe my ears. I asked her if she was familiar with his story of being baptized in the Holy Ghost. She said, *"No, I don't think I ever heard him give that part of his testimony since he's been here."* I then asked, *"You really don't know it?"* She replied, *"No."*

> You see, speaking in tongues can be faked, but, the power of God cannot! Just because someone says a salvation prayer doesn't mean they are now saved.

I briefly told her the same story I wrote you. Her eyes began to light up while her mouth dropped open. She stood there without words. She was experiencing the same type of power transferred over to her as he felt through the Holy Ghost when he was baptized in power. I smiled and started to turn away when she said, *"But, Marty, wait a minute, I'm not finished. When you prayed for me something different happened. That's why I asked."*

I turned to her in wonder, *"What do you mean something happened; something different?"* She said, *"I felt something else that's never happened to me before."* You talk about capturing my attention. *"What happened? What do you mean?"* She simply replied, *"I began to feel my fingertips tingle like they were being stuck with little needles as both my hands were going numb. Then it stopped as you stopped praying for me. What was that?"* I told her about how I was baptized in the Holy Ghost and shared the details of my reaction to the anointing. The Pastor's experience with the power of God was different from mine. He felt what some people call liquid love. The power I felt when baptized was going into my hands like electricity strong enough to make them tingle like sticking needles as they went numb. I could hardly believe it. The transfer of power from God through him, then from me, were two different demonstrations. This woman did not know our experiences with God. This was showing me we both had a different supply of the spirit of Christ. I was amazed. It was like turning on and then off a switch of some sort.

Here's another thing which makes it amazing. That power was coming into my hands for over two months before the stammering lips were ever given to me. Her experience revealed I was actually baptized in the Holy Ghost at the Greenville, SC crusade. If you remember, this demonstration showed up five days later. After all, is that not the very Words the Lord had spoken over me? Will God's own Words fall to the ground before He sees they are fulfilled? No, of course not. You see, speaking in tongues can be faked, but, the power of God cannot! Just because someone says a salvation prayer doesn't mean they are now saved. In the same way, just because someone says words which sound like the Heavenly language don't prove they are baptized in the Holy Ghost. Back at the crusade, I felt enough power that I thought my heart and chest might have burst if there was not a release. I also felt the power of the Holy Ghost similarly at that church the following June. The Heavenly language is a gift which comes from the power. The power is the first proof. (Yes, I know speaking in tongues will not only develop your spirit; but, it will bring more of God's power). We must remember it's a baptism of power, not a baptism of tongues. **"But ye shall receive power, after that the Holy Ghost is come upon you"** – Acts 1:8. The Holy Ghost came upon me for the first time that day at the crusade.

Elijah must come first

My Evangelist friend was for me the same thing Elijah was for Elisha. Elisha had to serve Elijah as an armor bearer (as a servant) before he was qualified before God to bear the mantle. My friend was my mentor. God used him to help position me spiritually in a place I could not reach by myself. This is a biblical pattern. In Mark 9:12 the Word tells us that Elijah must come first. In Matthew 11:14, Jesus said this about John the Baptist, **"This is Elijah."** That was why John the Baptist was sent before Jesus. You see, I had my suspicions before I met him I would be called to that type of work. I never felt too much like a typical pastor. I knew something was missing. The idea of being a pastor never felt right to me. I felt like an evangelist. Serving God under him seemed to strengthen my spirit in a stronger way. It awakened and energized my spirit man like nothing else could. I could feel the anointing was there for me to do what God was asking. It was stronger. That's another way I knew I was following after what God had for my life. I grew to see I was supposed to have and walk in that kind of anointing. In Numbers 11:16 we read where God commanded Moses to gather seventy of the leaders of the people together. Then in verse 17, God said, *"I will come down and talk with thee there: and I will take of the spirit which is upon thee, and will put it upon them."* That's what happened with Elisha. He took hold of Elijah's mantle after God took him away. His mantle represented the spirit Elijah received from God. Then John the Baptist came in that same spirit. I come to find out this was what my service was all about. I was to receive a transfer of the same type anointing/spirit which God gave him.

You have to know what belongs to you to receive it. This wasn't something my mentor could give. He couldn't give this to me any more than Elijah could give it to Elisha. You must receive it from God, not man. You have to know it belongs to you. Faith needs to be a factor. You're the one that must take it. Do you remember how Jesus was rejected in His hometown? Through their lack of faith and unbelief He could do very little there (Mark 6:1-6). There are many places in the Word where Christ Jesus said it was their faith which was doing the work. Elisha knew it was up to him to take the mantle. It wasn't about the man. It fell from heaven. John the Baptist knew what he was to do and why he was sent. I knew what God was showing me. I soon grew to a place in Him where I knew it was mine to take. I could see it by faith. Faith became the substance of the very thing I hoped for. Through faith, it became real to me. Just like His hometown; I had to take it by faith just as the sick had to take their healing. If you know you're calling, find and serve the Lord under someone who carries that type of anointing/spirit. Connect with it. Invest into it. Then wait for God's timing.

The double portion

Elisha carried a double portion anointing. He said in 2 Kings 2:9, **"I pray thee, let a double portion of thy spirit be upon me."** Here we can see the same word "spirit" being used again. It's used this way to identify a certain supply. As a Christian, we have the supply of the spirit of Christ. As you read on through you can see this mantle gave Elisha the ability to perform twice as many works as his mentor Elijah did. Now that takes me to another point. Christ Jesus said in John 13:16, **"The servant is not greater than his lord."** Matthew 10:24 said he cannot be above his master. So, tell me, if Jesus said you cannot be greater than the one you serve under (and we know the Word of God cannot lie), then how does someone become greater than their leader? How was Elisha able to attain the double portion if he couldn't be greater than his mentor Elijah? While you're thinking, allow me to add this. Didn't Jesus say we will do greater works through Him?

I found the answer to this question while serving. God revealed how to do it. It's very simple. It deals with two things. One is the supply of the spirit of Christ. The other is the mantel. Every one of us has gifts. Serving under someone helps to bring out your gifts in a stronger way. Serving awakened and energized my spirit like nothing else could. I brought this up for one reason. Serving brings more development. In every church service I directed my faith to release everything which was in me to my mentor as he served. I did everything I could to help support him and make his job easier. I worked hard to be a servant. Allow me to point out some of what I mean. We were waiting outside a guest church just before a meeting was to begin. As we were standing out front I noticed his shoelace was untied. I stooped down and tied it back. As I did, I was thinking how John the Baptist said he wasn't worthy to even loose the sandals from off the Lords' feet. This was done by house servants just before they washed someone's feet. I then knew the Lord was talking to me. The Word says to do unto the least of these is to do it unto the Lord, Himself. That's when I in my heart knew the Lord was talking to me. ***"What you have done for him was the same as washing My feet."*** All you do should be done as to the Lord, though He may not be the one standing in front of you.

> Every one of us has gifts. Serving under someone helps to bring out your gifts in a stronger way. Serving awakened and energized my spirit like nothing else could. I brought this up for one reason. Serving brings more development.

Now back to the question I just asked you. If a servant cannot be greater than his lord, then how did Elisha gain the double portion anointing? How do you receive a double measure? It will come through being a servant. The thing to remember about being a servant is duty comes before self. Here is what the Lord said to me. The first measure is the mantle of God for your call. Each calling may be a little different. There's an anointing for healing. There's an anointing for deliverance. There's also a different grace for those who minister to children or to the broken hearted. No one person can do everything. We, as a whole, make up the body of Christ. There is a different anointing for different callings. The mantle is what brings the first portion or measure. The second is your supply. This reflects your spiritual growth or development. That's where you are in your walk with God. Every time I gave of myself I was making a deposit into the spirit realm. I was using my faith to daily attach supply after supply to the mantle my mentor carried. Before too long the Lord told me, **"One day I will give you of that mantle (spirit), and you will receive back everything you have invested over to it; I will return all you've given to me."** Not only do you receive the mantle of the Lord for your call, but; you get back everything you have invested. That's the double portion! I was responsible for the level of measure and supply I would one day receive. Do you see how this works? The weight of the portion which was coming back to me was based on the consistency and sincerity of my labor of love as I served. I controlled the outcome in the end; because I controlled the level of sacrifice from the beginning. Though I wasn't leading that ministry, I still had a supply to invest until the day God sent me out. This goes back to the Word. **"Lay not up for yourselves treasures upon earth, where moth and rust doth corrupt, and where thieves break through and steal: But lay up for yourselves treasures in heaven where thieves do not break through nor steal."** – Matthew 6:19-20

> The first servant took the five talents and invested them so they became ten. The second servant was given two and grew them to four. This is a picture of a double measure. Both of these servants were commended for their act of service, but the third was not. Do you know why? He walked in fear and not faith. This man buried his master's talent.

Don't bury your talent

There's another topic which relates to this. It's the parable of the talents. This story is found in Matthew 25:14-30. You may know it very well. To one servant, the master gave five talents, unto his second servant he gave two, and unto the third, he gave one. If you do a word search for "talent", you will find it's used to describe a measure or a measurement. The Word lists how each servant was given a different measure. We as believers have all been given a measure of faith (Romans 12:3). Here's a good way to look at it. Your measure is your supply. The first servant took the five talents and invested them so they became ten. The second servant was given two and grew them to four. This is a picture of a double measure. Both of these servants were commended for their act of service, but the third was not. Do you know why? He walked in fear and not faith. This man buried his master's talent. This servant was disobedient to the job he was given. If he wasn't sure how to trade he could have followed the leading of those with more experience just as Elisha followed Elijah.

I brought this up because of something the Lord said to me. If I'm not mistaken, the Lord spoke this to me just before I began writing the books. While in my prayer room one afternoon I recalled some things I'd learned, along with much of my testimony. There were so many things coming back to my attention that I felt His goodness and mercy in a way as I rarely understood it before. I thought about when He healed me. I put into remembrance the liberty the truth of His Word brought to me. Then, I thought about His Glory. I thought on His call to preach and much more. All I wanted was to be used. I wanted to see what His power could do. I wanted to start serving His call so bad I almost couldn't stand waiting any longer. Then the Lord said to me, *"If you keep these things to yourself, you have buried My talent."* The bottom line is this; serve and keep serving. Do all you can do. Don't quit. Don't give up or give in no matter how bad it gets. A loyal savant won't bury his talent. When the day comes where I'm able to stand before the Lord I want to hear what the good servants heard. **"Well done, thou good and faithful servant."**

I want to be faithful with what the Lord has entrusted to me. Do you? I know there are those who will disagree with much of what I have written. I understand that. I also understand some people don't hear what is being said. They only hear what they can understand. You see, some people don't want the truth no matter what the truth may be. They want the truth as they perceive it to be. I hope these truths and experiences will help you hear from God for yourself. My heart is that no one will assume I'm trying to boast of myself. So, I hope while reading this book you have looked at your own life. I hope my life experiences can help you to relate to your own. May each example help draw your attention to what God has and is doing in your life.

What if we miss the deeper things of God because our idea of Him doesn't fit with who He really is? Only you know if God is speaking to you and moving in your life. I must follow God where my assignment is concerned. I know that I know the Lord. If you know the Lord, it's because He has made an investment in your life. We all have a supply if we are in Christ. The more we serve and encounter Him, the more of a supply there will be. Every encounter with God is a deposit of His life in us. This makes us responsible to serve the kingdom. So, whatever you do, please hear me. Don't keep Him to yourself. Be that witness you know you should be. Don't hide or hold back your supply. Don't bury your talent.

CHAPTER 16
THE CHRIST FACTORS

AS CONCERNING SPIRITUAL THINGS, I HAVE SEEN THREE IMPORTANT FACTORS AT work; the source, the force, and the course. I believe each one helps bring direction concerning the will of God for everyone's life. I have seen how it can influence God's call. The Lord has shown them to me as I surrendered, served the church, and studied the life of John the Baptist and Jesus' ministry. It doesn't matter who you are or what God saved you from. Everyone's a candidate for being used in the work of God. We all have something we can do. The Great Commission is the great leveler. No one should ever assume they aren't good enough to be used by God. Every born again believer qualifies.

No one that has ever been sent into this world was sent without God planning it to be so. This applies to one's life both physically and spiritually. If you're here now, then you should be here now. A life cannot exist without reason or purpose. Your life is not an accident. God has a plan for you. If you want to find out what the meaning of life is, look to Christ Jesus. He is the author and the finisher of our life just as much as He is for our faith. A life living without purpose is usually a life that's dreaded. The world is full of unhappy people. You don't have to be one of them. Because of "Finding Power to Live Ministries" ®, I'm able to see things differently. The word "LIVE" now has special meaning for me. Through Christ, I'm "**Living In V**ictory **E**very-day."

Too many individuals think they're not called of God unless they're a preacher. This is far from the truth. I happen to know ministers will tell you everyone is called to do something for God in one way or another. Besides, if you have a salvation testimony, then you have a message which needs to be preached. The greatest call anyone can receive in this life from God is His salvation call.

Factor one: Know God's Word

The Word of God is the first place to start. It's the basis for all truth and always will be. It's our source of truth, for power, and for life. When everything in your life either falls apart or fails the Word of God will not. In the beginning was the Word (John 1:1). The "Word Factor" must come first. In looking back over my story that's what you'll see. I didn't begin experiencing and knowing God until His Word was a working factor. The Word will bring to focus purpose for your life. Connecting with His Word will connect you with Him. This is also true where it concerns salvation. 1 Peter 1:23 states, we are born of the Word. It's very important to know God's Word. There are different Bible translations, Christian books, and study formats. It doesn't matter what you use as long as you can understand it enough to hear from God through it. Always remember that hearing is the key. I prefer the King James Version. If you're looking for a study source may I suggest something? The best Bible study resource you can ever trust in is the Holy Spirit. He is our teacher. With Him, all types of study resources can help open the door for God to get into your life. Knowing the Word will aid us in knowing more about God the Father, His Son Christ Jesus, and the Holy Spirit. The Word will help you gain a better understanding of who you're called to be. You just have to look for God to see how He might be reaching out to you. It will always be a little different for everyone. But it will always be based on the Word. That's what makes it up-close and personal. There must be some kind of relationship in place. Following after His Word is the best way to know He's talking to you. This, however, won't happen without you really seeking Him for yourself.

> When everything in your life either falls apart or fails the Word of God will not. In the beginning was the Word (John 1:1). The "Word Factor" must come first.

In the Gospel of John 1:23 we read where John the Baptist said, **"I am the voice of one crying in the wilderness, Make straight the way of the lord, as said the prophet Esaias** (which being interpreted is Isaiah)." He was making reference to chapter and verse 40:3 in the book of Isaiah. **"The voice of** him that crieth in the wilderness, Prepare ye the way of the Lord, make straight in the desert a highway for our God."

John's father was a priest (Luke 1:5). I happen to think John the Baptist was familiar with the scriptures because of his upbringing. He must have known about the Christ which was to come. This is how he may have come to know who he was. He knew the Word. I believe he found this out because his focus was looking for what God was about to do next. Can you imagine what it must have been like for John the day he saw and understood it was he that God was talking about? That it was he the verse spoke of so long ago. That he was the one which would open the gate (the truth of God's Word) and make a way for the shepherd to enter in (John chapter 10). If you're ever going to know the God of the Word you must know His Word in the same way. Make it intimate. You have to know He wrote it just for you. You have to see God talking directly to you by His Word. The Word of God must become personal and relevant to you and your life right now. You must first know the Word. It must become logical. It's one thing to just read about something; but, it's another thing to know God's talking directly to you!

Factor two: Knowing Christ

The second factor is the "Christ factor." Christ is our life, wisdom, and the power to overcome this world. To know who you are as a Christian is to know what you have in God being your Heavenly Father. This is what I saw in 1999 through the handmade parchment. In Philippians 3:10 it is written, **"That I may know him, and the power of his resurrection...."** To know Him is to know the Christ that's in you. To know the power of His resurrection is to know the hope of His Glory which lives and is at work in you. That's why the Apostle Paul said, **"For I determined not to know anything among you, save Jesus Christ, and him crucified."** (1 Corinthians 2:2). Every believer should strive to know this. Furthermore, every believer should be sent by the Lord to this world in the spirit of Christ with the power of God. This is how God sent John the Baptist. He was sent in the spirit of Elijah and the power of God (Luke 1:17, John 1:25). We not only need the spirit of Christ but, we need the power of the Holy Ghost. It's very important to not only know who is anointing you but to know what it is in you that He is anointing. If you reflect back to my testimony, you can see how my life was being made new to me time and time again. Through the work of the spirit of Christ and of God, I found His mighty hand functioning in my life. Revival became a lifestyle for me instead of a grouping together of meetings someone might attend at a church. By having day to day interaction with the Lord and by being a servant, God will identify what your supply in Christ Jesus is and help to enable you to follow His Spirit and His work for your life.

The Church is full of people who have never made it to the second factor. They live in the first because it's easier. This next factor cannot come to you but through death to self, devotion, and discipline. I also think there are those who are afraid they will be seen as being religious. Many become guilty of allowing this fear to drive them to the point of burying what God has invested in them. Most people who make it to the second factor have a unique mindset; they see things differently. They're not afraid of the sacrifice that's required for every day. I say that because this strength grows and thrives first from behind closed doors. If you're not real with God in the secret places, then you're not real with Him at all. I'm not saying some people have arrived at a place of perfection. NO! We all need God to work on us. We all have more we can surrender. I don't know what keeps so many from breaking through. I'm not where I need to be but, I broke through. I think it's sad. They miss more than they will ever know. As I think back over the years, I believe there aren't very many people in the body of Christ who I've met which have broken through to that place with God. Those who break through are easy to spot. They are sometimes called the remnant Church. They stand out in a crowd. It's easier to see there's something different about them. They don't talk like a typical Christian. Plus, they carry a different spirit on their life. Somehow, they just don't look like the people of the world even when they aren't doing anything. These people are anointed.

Factor three: the Visitation

The third factor is the "Visitation factor." This is truly a rare experience. It's a place of invitation. You can't work your way up to it. I know, I didn't. The truth is I'm looking forward to seeing more. I expect to one day. All I can say is it's something the Lord chooses to do. I wish I could tell you more. Throughout the Word of God we see one account after another where a visitation took place. I am convinced that John the Baptist had a visitation. In John 1:33 we read, **"And I knew him not: but he that sent me to baptize with water, the same said unto me, Upon whom thou shalt see the Spirit descending, and remaining on him, the same is he which, baptizeth with the Holy Ghost."** In the words, **"he that sent me to baptize with water, the same said unto me"**, we can see John gives an account of a visitation from God. Was it the Lord that visited him by His Spirit? Was it an angel, or a vision of one of the prophets? We may not know exactly who sent him or how it was done; but, we know it took place. The way he referred to it was enough to tell that it was coming from the Lord. I think if God was using a person alive at the time we would have a record of the details of the event, like the name of the one who talked with John. Personally, I think it was an angel. After all, it was an angel which visited Joseph and Mary in regards to the birth of Jesus. Up to this point the Holy Ghost had not been sent or given to men yet (John 7:39). Another reason I believe that is because, it was also an angel which visited and feed Jesus after He came out of His 40 day fast being tempted of the devil in the desert. Just like in Old Testament times, angels were still ministering to the people.

I am blessed to have had my own visitation. I also happened to be fortunate enough to witness another visitation in the life of someone else. It came with emotional healing. Are you familiar with Luke 4:18 where Jesus said, **"The Spirit of the Lord is upon me"**? One of the things He said was, **"he hath sent me to bind up the brokenhearted."**

Healing of a broken heart came to her. It was during an altar call I gave where I saw something strange. A young woman was being escorted by two others, one on each arm. The lady could hardly stand without help. She was crying uncontrollably. I immediately discerned what was happening. A few of them thought something was wrong, like a heart attack or stroke. I knew what was happening because it happened to me. It was about forty minutes before she could tell me what occurred. She said, *"I saw a vision. The hand of the Lord was holding a needle and thread and....He was sewing up my broken heart."*

> The church is full of people who have never made it to the second factor. They live in the first because it's easier. This next factor cannot come to you but through death to self, devotion, and discipline. I also think there are those who are afraid they will be seen as being religious.

This is the same picture being described in that verse. In every case of visitation one thing is always present. The knowledge of God is given to you with such intensity that it overtakes you! For the Church to grow in their spirit, they must grow in the knowledge of God in Christ. It's time for the Church to grow in their spiritual development. If I could pray one prayer for you and your church it would be for a visitation.

The first factor deals with growing in the Word. It's the source factor. The Word is the source of all truth just as God is the source of all life. If you ever want to grow, His Word must become your source and not this world. The bottom line is you must develop a relationship with God. You won't have the ability to do this without having His Word. He's more than our creator; He's Father. If you don't know His Word, you don't know Him. A relationship must first be developed with Him to see development take place in you. The second factor is in two parts; the spirit of Christ and the Spirit of God. This factor is the force factor. This factor involves you being a servant. It's the equipping and anointing stage of your walk with God. Just as John came in the spirit of Elijah and the power of God, so we must walk in the power of the spirit of Christ and in the anointing of the Holy Ghost. That's the way Jesus came. Acts 10:38 says, **"How God anointed Jesus of Nazareth with the Holy Ghost and with power."** This is how we also must come. We need to not only be developed in this new nature but, we need to be baptized in the Holy Ghost with power. The third factor is a place of visitation. I also see it as something which sets the course for our life. Did you notice that John's visitation came with God's invitation? This factor also deals with being sent. Look at my story. The visitation came to me after God gave me the call. John was sent. Jesus was sent. So was the Holy Ghost. Just because it may take several years before your ready doesn't mean you're not set apart. After all, what are you going to say? What are you taking with you? It's not who you are that God is sending. He's sending Jesus. That's who He's making you to be. It's about the investment He's making within you. We are His vessels. God's not sending a man or woman; He's sending a message. He's sending Christ in spirit form in and under the power of His Spirit. God's not going to send you until He has something in you to send; for many are called (invited) but few are chosen (favored). If God is sending you, then you are being favored.

> It's not who you are that God is sending. He's sending Jesus. That's who He's making you to be. It's about the investment He's making within you. We are His vessels. God's not sending a man or woman; He's sending a message. He's sending Christ in spirit form in and under the power of His Spirit.

CHAPTER 17
BREAKING THE CHAOS

I CAN DESCRIBE THE TERM CHAOS BY ANOTHER WORD: A CURSE. I SEE CHAOS AS THE reflux reaction of a curse which is operating in and over a person's life. Breaking the chaos is stopping a curse. I think most curses, if not all, are spiritual in origin though much of their results may show up in the natural. In *Dead to Sin*, I have much to say regarding our God-given right to walk in dominion in and over the earth. Having the blessing of the Lord on your life is where dominion starts. I believe the best way to understand more about dominion is by learning more about God's blessing. In the beginning, Adam and Eve were blessed by God to govern the Earth. They were given dominion over it. But, through their act of sin, the dominion they had was lost. Their sin released a curse upon the earth (Genesis 3:17). Breaking the hold or control of a curse is where taking back dominion starts. The curse breeds chaos, but blessing will bring dominion back.

Most people understand a curse is the opposite of a blessing. The loss of God's blessing is what came to Adam and Eve as a result of their disobedience. When they lost dominion, they gained the curse. The curse is the devil's counterpart to God's blessing. That's why I see chaos as being the counterpart to dominion. I believe much of what may go wrong in life is connected to that curse Adam and Eve first brought upon the Earth so long ago. We have to keep a watchful eye over everything that's going on in our lives. You may think of chaos as being something which extends beyond a few things here and there that have to be fixed or managed. But, I think that's where dominion can start. It can be found in the smaller things of life. A good example of this is no matter who you are you still must sweep, mop, or vacuum your house from time to time. After God placed Adam in the Garden of Eden, He commanded him **"to dress it and to keep it"** (Genesis 2:15). The act of taking dominion doesn't just include the day to day details of life but, that's how it began with Adam. But, there's another side to it.

When I refer to the other side of dominion, I'm talking about never having a break from struggling with life because it seems everything around you falls apart or goes wrong every time you turn around. I know of people that look like they can never find peace or joy in their life. Some people find it hard to catch a break. There's some kind of drama going on all the time. Just talking with them can pull you down. I also know of people who are accident prone or constantly losing something and can't seem to stop that "chaos" from happening no matter what they do. That's like taking one step forward then two steps back. Perhaps you've seen this in others. Maybe it's happening to you. We've all had circumstances turn or change for the negative before. It's as if these circumstances have a mind of their own. Perhaps money is the best example of all. I know of a time when I thought things were so far out of control that I might not be able to put them back into order. It's as if there's some form of intelligence behind it all. There are also some people which say things like, *"It's something all the time!"* What about this statement? *"If I didn't have bad luck, I wouldn't have any luck at all."* The devil can even use chaos as a door to gain access to your life. It's important to not lose self-control. The first step to discipleship is self-discipline. If you're tired of dealing with a mess all the time start using the name of Jesus. It's time to rise up and take hold of the life God's promised. That life's available by the power of Christ in your inner man. When we take hold of the power of Christ, we're taking hold of dominion. The kingdom of God is within you.

> The devil can even use chaos as a door to gain access to your life. It's important to not lose self-control. The first step to discipleship is self-discipline. If you're tired of dealing with a mess all the time start using the name of Jesus.

Let's take a look at the words **"to dress it and to keep it."** The timeline we see here in the Word indicates this was before God put Adam to sleep to make him a companion. This was before Eve's time. That's what's so interesting about this verse. Here we have God putting a perfect man into a perfect place yet Adam still had to do something to fix it up and to keep it in order!

The very words which come to mind when I read **"to dress it and to keep it"** are "to put it (the garden) in order and keep it together." When I was a single man keeping my house clean and in order was easy because I was the only one living there at the time. Now that I'm married with children, it's a harder job. Keeping your life in order is something everyone does every day. Here's another example. Do you not take a shower or bath, wash your hair and brush your teeth every day? What about eating right and exercising to improve your health? This is to dress and to keep your life, is it not? That's just what Adam was required to do with the garden. If you look, it can be seen in everyday circumstances of life. You might now ask, *"Do you mean to tell me the Garden of Eden was not in full order; therefore, God required Adam to take charge over it?"* Yes. That's a strange idea because we've all assumed that to not be so. Can you think of why that is? It's because we have always thought of the curse Adam released being that which caused all the problems of the world in the first place. It is written in Genesis 3:17 **"in sorrow shall thou eat of it all the days of thy life."** These words, **"in sorrow,"** means God's command to Adam was he should toil the soil of the earth for food. This is very interesting because the command for Adam to dress and keep the garden was given before the curse entered into the world. Which means every problem in life isn't based on spiritual warfare. Sometimes things just happen.

God didn't wait for the curse to enter; He gave the command **"to dress it and to keep it"** in the beginning. The Word of God is clear where Adam's job in the Garden was concerned. So think about this. What if God speaking this command to Adam is how dominion began? What if dominion's been right in front of our face and in our hands this entire time and we simply haven't seen it? The truth is God's still speaking to us today; commanding us **"to dress it and to keep it"** just as He spoke to Adam in the beginning.

Walking in dominion is your kingdom right as a believer. I've now grown to a place where I see walking in dominion as being a kingdom work. Yet, most believers may never recognize the work of the kingdom when they see it. Every time you recognize the hand of God working in your life you are seeing the advancement of the kingdom of God. Seeing the advancement of God's kingdom is not only seeing the kingdom of God being built up but, you're seeing dominion being enforced.

John 3:1-11 tells us the story of how the Pharisee Nicodemus came to Jesus in the night. I found something written here which caught my attention. Nicodemus said, **"We know that thou art a teacher come from God: for no man can do these miracles that thou doest, except God be with him."**

In verse 3 Jesus said, *"Verily, verily, I say unto thee, Except a man be born again, he cannot see the kingdom of God."* What has doing miracles and seeing the kingdom of God have to do with each other? What do they have in common? His answer to Nicodemus regarding those miracles shows us this is a kingdom work. To see a miracle is seeing the advancement of the kingdom of God. Now, here is another point. Jesus said, *"I do nothing except that which I see my Father doing"* (John 5:19). Before you can see dominion, you must first see the kingdom of God. But, to see the kingdom of God you must see the work God is doing. And seeing the work of God comes by watching God move and joining in with Him when a need is present. It's by being a servant. Seeing and hearing is the key. But, we don't always watch with the natural eyes. Seeing is not always believing. Faith is our seeing.

Don't just sit back and watch. Join in with what the Father is doing. Get involved in the service of a local church. It's a good place to start. A local body of believers will help you. But, you must have a relationship with God to recognize when He is moving. Otherwise, you won't know His direction. There must be a personal connection between you and the Lord. However, this won't happen without your obedience and surrender. Perhaps that was why I experienced God so many times. That's how I was able to tell the difference between what was coming from God and what could be dismissed as circumstances. This is how we build a relationship with the Father. Building a relationship with Him is how we walk with Him. It is a daily interaction. This is why I felt impressed to include much of my testimony. God wants you to walk with Him as well. He wants to use you. We all have a part to take in His work. There's room for everyone. When was the last time you remember seeing God's hand at work in your life? When was the last time you saw the kingdom of God?

"And I appoint unto you a kingdom, as my Father hath appointed unto me" – Luke 22:29

Now, one last thing; do you understand Luke 22:29? Take another look. Did you notice what Jesus said? He didn't appoint us to the kingdom. The kingdom has been appointed to us! The Father didn't give us to the kingdom, He gave the kingdom to us. The authority of the kingdom wasn't placed over us. The authority was given to us! That's the blessing. The kingdom isn't over you. The kingdom of God is within you. His blessing is our inheritance.

CHAPTER 18
WE ALL HAVE A PART IN GOD'S WORK

I HAVE WITNESSED, FIRST HAND, THE WORK OF GOD IN MY LIFE AS WELL AS IN THE life of many others. I have watched God break one curse after another, time and time again. It has come through bringing things like peace, hope, and physical healing in the lives of others around me. One thing I know is this, the Father loves us all. He wants to make an increase in our life. He wants to bless us and restore our spirit, soul, and body. One of the earliest experiences I can recall is regarding a cousin. After graduating high school, we hung around so much we were like brothers. We both shared a connection only time could bring. He was not a church person, and I knew that. Don't get me wrong. Only God knows if someone's saved or not; but, there was no spiritual fruit in his life that I could see at this time. I witnessed no hunger for the things of God.

In prayer one day, I came across a verse that took hold of me. 2 Corinthians 4:3 says, **"But if our gospel be hid, it is hid to them that are lost"**. The NIV version uses the word **"blind"** instead of **"lost"**. In the next verse, you can see it's the god of this world (the devil) that's making people blind. That's when I saw myself using this to break the power of the enemies hold over my cousin. I used my faith to reach out to him. With each prayer, I pictured him standing before me. I could almost see him living with a pair of blinders over his eyes. You know the kind which some folks like to use while they're sleeping. This made it easier to direct my focus. I reached out by faith. I envision myself taking hold of those blinders in the act of pulling them away while confessing the verse over him. I also put my faith on Matthew 16:19. It says, **"And I will** give unto thee the keys of the kingdom of heaven: and whatsoever thou shalt bind on earth shall be bound in heaven: and whatsoever thou shalt loose on earth shall be loosed in heaven."* I couldn't tell you how many times I pointed my faith as though I was pointing my finger at his situation. I would command over and over, *"In the name of Jesus, I lose you from the blinders of the devil and bind his hold over your mind."*

One day I got a phone call after midnight; it was my cousin. I didn't yet know that by the way he was acting. He was frazzled and in a panic. It took a few moments to calm him down enough to find out who it was. I then asked him, *"What's wrong? Has something happened?"* He simply responded, *"The devil is in my room!"* All I could say back was, *"What?"* He raised his voice a little louder. *"Man, the devil is in my room!!"* After a pause I said the only thing I could say. *"The devil…is in…your room?"* *"Yes!"* he replied. I'd been asleep for over two hours when the call came in. This really caught me off-guard. This was the last thing I thought I would ever hear from anyone. At that point, he began to go into detail to describe where he was in the room and where the spirit was alone with what it was doing. I said, "that spirit" because I knew it wasn't the devil; just an unclean spirit. *"Please pray for me. I need your help,"* was all he was left saying. I wasn't sure what to say. This was the first time I was used of God this way. As I was preparing to pray, I heard God speak to me, ***"You have been praying for the blinders to loose from his eyes. Well, they are now gone."*** The Word of God is powerful. A prayer released by faith is also an amazing thing.

Another of my earlier encounters of God's work took place when I needed help. I was sick with a sinus infection. I'd been sick for around a week or so. The back of my throat was sore. I was beginning to see some bleeding. It was Wednesday just days before Christmas in 1997. The church was observing the Lord's Supper. I didn't care how bad I felt. I wanted to partake. Besides, I didn't want to miss a church service because I might miss God. All I wanted to do was seek the Lord and be near Him. As the service began the pastor read from 1 Corinthians 11:23-28. He taught this from the point of forgiveness through the blood of Jesus. Soon I found myself being led by the Spirit of God to the next few verses. The next two dealt with the danger of not observing the body of the Lord while taking communion. Paul stated that many became sick or even died because of it. The drink symbolized the blood of the Lord while the bread stood for His body. I saw the pastor's message was directed to the facts concerning the blood; but what about the body? That's when it dawned on me something was missing from his message. He covered the facts about the blood, but not the Lord's body. I started to run everything through my mind when I saw the truth. I heard the voice of the Lord speak these very words, ***"By my stripes were you healed."*** His words hit my soul. I could now see the Word, where it concerns His body, as it should be seen. Jesus said, ***"This is my body."*** Taking that broken piece of bread was now no different to me than taking the very body of the Lord Himself! All of a sudden, healing became logical and no idea could break it from my grasp. I took the Lord's Supper knowing what it truly meant.

The next day, as I awoke, my throat was worse. That mattered not. I continued in prayer throughout the day while at work. Every time the pain would re-enter my throat I confessed the Word and believed. It wasn't easy all the time. My situation challenged my trust in God's Word. Whenever that happened, I thought back to the very moment when the Lord spoke to me. I remembered what I felt. I remembered how logical healing had become. You see, sometimes it seems our body doesn't want to respond. At times we have to force this decision. That goes back to my definition of faith. Faith is "Something that forces a decision apart from or in opposition to reason."

> Sometimes it seems our body doesn't want to respond. At times we have to force this decision. That goes back to my definition of faith. Faith is "Something that forces a decision apart from or in opposition to reason."

The next morning I awoke not thinking about how my body felt the day before. As I prayed over my breakfast the revelation of His healing came back to me just as fresh as it was two days before. As I continued to pray I took hold of the words the Lord spoke. I was feeding on His Word just as much as I was about to feed on my waffles. I pinched off the corner of one, picked up my glass of orange juice, and was about to begin taking communion. I then felt a strange sensation. A weight close around my neck like the hand of the Lord was taking holding of me. That's when I felt the pain being pulled out of my throat like it was attached to a string. Then the pressure around my throat eased off, lifted from me and was gone. I was healed!

This next story occurred a year later. At that time I was still learning about the power of Christ where healing is concerned. Nevertheless, I was soon to see the hand of God work once again. This time it was in the life of my two-year-old niece. She had been sick for a number of days. My brother had taken her to the doctor twice with no results. I come to find out that she was running a fever of a 102. If her condition didn't change soon, they were taking her to the hospital. This was where I come in. It was Friday. I was off work and babysat her all day while the family worked. It was very easy to see she was sick. Instead of running around getting into things, all she wanted to do was either sleep or sit in my lap while I held her. Sometime after lunch, I started feeling a strong pull to pray over her condition. I knew it was Christ in me which was doing the pulling. It was a strange feeling and still new to me. However, I followed the Lord's pulling. It wasn't a little or short type of prayer. It was a steady and soaking kind. It wasn't loud or pushy, but firm with the substance of faith mixed in. I could feel what seemed like my spirit becoming warm and strong. I could feel the power of Christ in my focus. It's difficult to describe. Godly motivation is different than human motivation. I continued in prayer for some time, then, I felt a release. It was like finding rest and peace for my soul over her condition. Soon, my brother came home from work, and I was on my way home.

Sunday morning after church I walked down to the nursery to find my niece running and playing again. It was easy to see she was feeling much better. The next day I asked my brother how she was. *"Well, I guess you remember me telling you that she was taken to the doctor twice and wasn't getting any better."* I responded, *"Yea."* Then he said, *"Friday, when you came over, she was running a fever of 102."* He then stopped with a puzzled look on his face and said, *"But, by Friday night…she was alright. Her fever was gone."*

There was something strange about that experience. In the timeline of my story, this took place when I wasn't baptized in the Holy Ghost yet. How was the power of God available to me? If we can only move in miracle-working power after the Holy Ghost anoints us then why was power there for her? One thing is very clear. She couldn't pull herself together and believe God for healing. The child was only two years of age. So, how did it happen? I'm asking you this because many circles of faith that hold to the baptism of the Holy Ghost believe this baptism must come first. They believe there is no real power without it. If I wasn't baptized in the Holy Ghost then how was she healed? How was God able to use me? I will answer these questions by pointing out two things. The first has been included in my book, *Dead to Sin*. In the tenth chapter of the Gospel of Matthew we read that Christ Jesus gave His disciple's power. This was long before He sent them God's Spirit. They were doing the work of God but didn't have the baptism of the Holy Ghost yet. God used me in the same way. I had the power of Christ though I wasn't baptized by the Holy Spirit yet. The Word shows us Christ Jesus is the power of God. And, that the Christ of Jesus lives in you if you are a true believer. This is the hope we now have in Him. This power deals with dominion. This is kingdom authority. Finding this and living through the power of Christ in you is the heart of "Finding Power to Live ministries."

The second point which supports this power can be found in a story contained in the book of Acts. **"Then Philip went down to the city of Samaria, and preached Christ unto them. And the people with one accord gave heed unto those things which Philip spake, hearing and seeing the miracles which he did. For unclean spirits, crying with loud voice, came out of many that were possessed with them: and many taken with palsies, and that were lame, were healed."** (Acts 8:5-7). As you read down to verse 14-17 you see that Peter and John heard of this work and went down to them. After arriving, they saw that none of them were baptized in the Holy Ghost. They, therefore, prayed for them, laid their hands upon them so they would all receive. Here is a picture of two types of work. Philip ministered the same power that was seen being done throughout the four Gospels. Though there was no baptism of the Spirit of God, there was power. Philip was preaching the name of Christ while the Apostles preached the Holy Ghost. The first part may be the most important; it's by knowing Christ personally. The second deals with living for Christ; it's by knowing the power of His resurrection. Wherever Christ is properly preached and believed there will be power. Where there is power, there are miracles. There is power in the name of Jesus.

> I could feel the power of Christ in my focus. It's difficult to describe. Godly motivation is different than human motivation. I continued in prayer for some time, then, I felt a release. It was like finding rest and peace for my soul over her condition.

Every time we encounter God working in our life we experience a miracle. The truth is the encounter alone is a miracle in itself. This is so because every encounter reveals Christ in a real way instead of Him only being a thought you might have had or an idea from another individual. Jesus isn't ancient history, His alive today and forever. God must be real to you. What He can do won't become real for your life until He becomes real in your life. If the life that's in you is of God's life, this world (earth) will respond to it; because it's not following you but God. It's following what God put in you. *"Being alive to God means those things that are alive to God are alive to us."* In this, you see for yourself the Holy Spirit is there watching over you. All we need to do is walk with Him and respond to His prodding. If you are willing to surrender and be a servant, then those things which respond to Christ will start responding to the Christ in you.

My next story is one of healing for the heart and spirit. My family planned to take a trip to Tennessee to visit my sister and her family. It was Memorial Day. She recently moved into a new apartment and wanted everyone to see it. Around lunch, we all went out to eat. After ordering, it became obvious that something was bothering the waitress. She was very slow. Our orders began arriving incorrectly. She also gave them back to the wrong people. No one was saying much to her at the time. I knew it was about to come to a head. There was one or two in the family known for speaking their mind. I began feeling sorry for her. I knew what was coming if she didn't improve quickly. Just then a strong pull came over my heart for her. I didn't know the woman. I knew I would never see her again. I lived nearly six hours away. Nevertheless, I knew she needed for someone to take the time to reach out to her. Upon returning to our table, it was apparent that she already knew what we thought about her service. Her voice and facial expressions gave it away. I called out to her, hoping to cut off anyone from having a chance to speak first. I asked, *"Can I pray for you?"* She stopped and just looked at me. Then turning to the others, she asked, *"Is he serious?"* My father bent his head over slightly and responded, *"Yes. He's serious."* I surprised her. The look in her eyes told the story. She was looking for hope but hadn't found it yet. I took her hand and prayed. She lifted her head and gave back a light smile, turned and went back to work. We all began to see a change in her, not only from the service but from her countenance. The tension was gone. Before we left, the young woman came up to our table and began apologizing for the bad service we received. Then she said, *"I want to thank you for praying for me. I grew up in church but, have been withdrawn for many years now. Yesterday, for the first time in years, I went back. I went to the altar at the end of the service and prayed. I needed to know God heard me and is here for me. I was at the last moments of deciding whether or not God had heard me...then you walked in. For a moment I'd given up, but now; I know God heard my prayer and is waiting for me to come back to Him."* Just when you think God is nowhere to be found, we find He's closer than ever.

The last story I have to relate marked me. It was one of correction from the Lord. I was rebuked for my lack of faith and love. I was at work. There was a young woman there who worked as a quality inspector for company production. Her office was upstairs, above the break room. I had gone on my break and she was on her way down to take hers. As she came in it was easy to see something was wrong. She moved slowly to the nearest chair and eased into it holding her lower back. Her actions revealed she must be in physical pain. I said nothing to her, I sat and observed. Within a minute, a strong motivation to pray for her began to rise. I shook it off. It soon returned. For months she and I had been discussing faith in God. She said she grew up going to church. She had faith in God; but, doubt in herself. She knew God was real; but, didn't think she deserved forgiveness. The problem was her lifestyle promoted this doubt. She wasn't living for the Lord. She shared some of her testimony with me. She was saved and baptized in the Holy Ghost with the gift of speaking in tongues at the age of eight. She knew better, yet for many years, she chose to stay away from God to live her own way. I suppose she thought it was easier or that she was stuck where she was. As I sat there, the Lord continued to pull on me. An entire list of things she was doing wrong played through my mind. It wasn't that I didn't want to pray for her. It wasn't that I didn't think God wanted to heal her hurt, body and soul. I wasn't judging her past. We all have one. I was thinking she might not receive from God because of her own lack of faith. I remember thinking, *"She's doing wrong and knows that. Does she even want to follow you?"* If something is able to block your faith, it will block you spiritually. Christ Jesus said, **"Be it done unto you according to thy faith."** So, my thoughts about her at that moment were, *"She probably doesn't even have the faith working in her now to believe that You want to touch her, Lord."* The Lord spoke to me. **"Do you have any idea how much I love her? Lay your hands upon her and pray for her!"** I was shaken to the very core of my being. I knew I was being rebuked. All I could say was, *"I have *to pray for you."* I reached out and began. I can't say I had very much confidence in myself or that prayer. What I knew I had was God. The fact that He spoke to me was an indicator something was about to happen. I could almost feel His watchful eyes hovering over us. It was like, by the act of releasing my prayer, I was releasing Him to do His work. In finishing, she looked at me as though a type of fear was holding her. I asked her, *"What's the matter?"* Her reply was, *"Why did you pray I wouldn't get cancer?"* I replied, *"What? I did? I don't know. I was just praying."* Sometimes I don't remember what I pray. She began to share the story of a family curse. There was a cancer which was being passed down from Aunt to niece over several generations. Her family was speaking this over her for years under the excuse of it being a warning. I had to calm her down a little. I said, *"Don't you worry about anything. I'm telling the truth when I say God just spoke to me. He told me to pray for you."* Later that afternoon our paths crossed. She came down with some paperwork with a smile across her face. I asked her how she was feeling. She smiled back. *"After you prayed for me, I went back to my office. I sat there and prayed myself. Your prayer really encouraged me. That's when I noticed the pain was gone. I believe God healed me."* Four months later, while driving to work, I recalled the event and wondered how things have gone for her. When I saw her, I asked. *"Do you remember the day I prayed for you about that back pain?"* She said, *"Oh, yes."* *"Well, how are you feeling now?"* I said. *"How have you been?"* She replied, *"Great. The pain never came back. I know God healed me."*

> Describing God's love is like telling someone not only what the Glory of God is like, but what it's all about. To be completely honest, when I saw God's glory, I saw love in the knowledge of who He is. There's nothing like His love. There's no one like Him. Nothing compares to Him.

This story opened my eyes to see two major things. The first is God loves us, all of us. He loves every person no matter what. To this day I feel I stand in a place of inadequacy where my knowledge of the love of God is concerned. Describing God's love is like telling someone not only what the Glory of God is like, but what it's all about. To be completely honest, when I saw God's glory, I saw love in the knowledge of who He is. There's nothing like His love. There's no one like Him. Nothing compares to Him. It's the one thing in my life I've come to see as truly real. It's Him; it's His love. God is love, and real love never fails! I long for the day I may once again embrace and be embraced by His powerful gaze. When I saw His face that day back in 1999, the knowledge of God changed things in me I didn't know could be changed. I ascertained an activation of my son-ship for a level

I never knew before. Knowing the love of God in Christ will activate life and power you didn't know you could walk in. Just as water and earth will bring life to a seed, the knowledge of Christ and of God will cause life to spring up in you. I don't know if it's even possible to reach the place where we can see our full potential manifest without seeing and experiencing who He is.

I learned the love God has for us is more real than I understood it to be. I'm not sure if you can understand how powerful His words about His love really were. I found so much life in His words they still live and resound in my heart and mind to this day. The effect on you is different when it's up-close and personal. It's more real when it comes to you first hand. God spoke to me as though all she needed to receive her healing was to know that He loved her. Think about all we've missed because we haven't come to know His love as it truly is. Think about what we may be capable of if we only knew what He knows about us and the life He has put in us. God knows we can do all things through Christ if only we would believe. For faith works best when it comes out of the knowledge of Christ and of God.

> The more I know Him the more I realize God believes in me more than I believe in Him. If you can say you don't know your full potential, then you must admit that God believes in you more than you believe in yourself.

Now, what I'm about to say next may be hard to grasp. But, I think God loves us more than we love ourselves. That brings me to the second thing I learned. I think God believes in us more than we believe in ourselves. When He called me out that day it was easy to see He believed in me more than I believed in myself. If that were not true, then I would've had the confidence I needed. I wouldn't have had any doubt in laying my hands on her. I would have known that the infirmity would leave. If you have listened to my heart throughout this book, there should be no doubt when I say I believe in Him. But, the more I know Him the more I realize God believes in me more than I believe in Him. If you can say you don't know your full potential, then you must admit that God believes in you more than you believe in yourself. Furthermore, if we really knew His love for us, we would have an understanding of His love for others. Most of us may know what the Word says about Him and His love; but, how developed are you in walking it out towards others? Do you actually know the power of Christ in you and what that can do? None of us do. None of us have seen our full potential in Christ. But, there is an encouraging side to it. We know there's more and can take hold of more if we continue to seek Him and only believe.

Knowing the Love of God in Christ may be the first step to knowing who we are as a living spirit. Discovering and living by Christ that's in you is finding power to live. There is another part to it though; it's the sacrifice that's required for living every day. In 2 Corinthians 4:17 we read, **"For our light affliction, which is but for a moment, worketh for us a far more exceeding and eternal weight of glory."** All that we endure, fight, and die to (or resist) in this life is only a light affliction in comparison to the power of Christ that's working and growing in our life by the spirit man. I happen to believe God uses our afflictions to activate who we are in Christ. The Apostle Paul said to endure hardship is the key to making Christ in you a working factor. The word **"weight"** in this verse is "authority." For the authority of Christ to increase, our response to "the flesh" and "the world" must decrease. Paul also said in Romans 8:10, when we force the body to take the spiritual position of death by not living for this world, our spirit man will have the liberty to then take more of the position of life. The life of Christ is what gives every believer their authority. If we want more authority, we must have less of self and more of Him.

CHAPTER 19
FORMED IN LIFE; FORMED IN POWER

AT THIS POINT, I KNOW YOU NOW HAVE SOME IDEA OF WHAT THE WORK OF GOD IS. As I've said in the beginning, the work of God is anything which builds and establishes the kingdom of Christ and of God. There's more to this than just believing Christ Jesus is the Son of God and understanding the work that was done by Him. We need to know who we are in Christ. It's about the work He's doing in us. It's extended to you by walking in His power to make a difference for the kingdom. Yet, many still do not walk in His power. Some may even have a heart for going to church. Some even have a heart for God. So, why is that? I think the main reason is they're not working in what the Father is calling them to do. Obedience is very important.

As for me, it all begins with having a relationship. The greatest revelation you can gain is the truth of being born again; that you are a child of God. This is reinforced by finding and living by the power of Christ through the anointing of the Holy Ghost. Just as Christ in you is the hope of glory. The kingdom of God that's within you is the authority of that same glory. It's your spirit within you and His authority that's at work in your spirit which is being built up. In Christ, you are daily being created **"after the power of an endless life"** (Hebrews 7:16). Just as Jesus is the fulfillment of the Old Testament, Christ in you is to be the fulfillment of the New. Just as the fulfillment of the Old Testament was completed by the manifestation of "The Son of God." So, the fulfillment of the New Testament will come by the manifestation of "the sons of God." Therefore, I believe the fullness of the work of God is the manifestation of Christ in the Church. We know there had to be a fulfillment of the Old Testament to move into the new. If there was a completion of the Old why would there not be a fulfillment of the New? I happen to believe the completion of the work of God is going to be the fulfillment of the New Testament. This moves over into a second part. This fulfillment may be what we lack to see the very thing which awaits the last days; that is "the rapture of the Church."

We are a chosen generation. We are being made into a royal priesthood in Christ (1 Peter 2:9). I said being made into this because He's still working on us. We are still growing. In 1 John 3:2 it says, **"Beloved, now are we the sons of God, and it doth not yet appear what we shall be: but we know that, when he shall appear, we shall be like him; for we shall see him as he is."** To be developed, you must know who it is you're to be developed into. This is the point I was trying to make about the knowledge of the love of God. The key to becoming more developed in Christ comes by the knowledge of the glory of God. Since God is love, I believe knowing God's love is the key to holding the knowledge of God's glory. That verse teaches no one becomes as He is until they first see who He is. Seeing Christ Jesus is seeing who God is making you to be. 1 Corinthians 13:12 says, **"For now we see through a glass, darkly; but then face to face: now I know in part; but then shall I know even as also I am known."** Right now we may only know Christ in part; but, God knows us after who Christ Jesus is right now, which is after our High priest in the order of Melchisedec.

Looking at who you are becoming in your spirit man is what 1 Corinthians 13:12 is referring to. We also find a similar verse in 2 Corinthians 3:18 which says, **"But we all, with open face beholding as in a glass the glory of the lord, are changed into the same image from glory to glory, even as by the Spirit of the Lord."** These two scriptures have been interrupted as referring to we being compared to the Bible. Yes, this can fit the part. However, we limit our understanding of the work of God by stopping with that. Do you know why? The Word became flesh (he's talking about being in body) and dwelt among us. Jesus, Himself, is what those verses are talking about. It's that simple. It's Christ Jesus we compare ourselves with. He's talking about your spirit, because of the state of being born again is not of the physical body, but of the spirit. What do you do when you look into a mirror? A mirror is designed to show what you reflect. Our lives should reflect the image of Christ.

The born again spirit is called the spirit of Christ. Furthermore, Jesus is in heaven with the Father but, Christ is in you. That life, His life, is in every born-again believer. That's the image your spirit man contains. That's what we're being changed into. This gives us a clearer understanding that it's Jesus this verse is talking about. How can I say it better than it's the Word of God that will activate Christ in you? As our Father God looks on us, He should see the image of His dear Son. I don't want to reflect Adam or this world. I don't want to reflect "church stuff." I want to reflect Christ in spirit form. This is why we need to be baptized by God's Spirit. The Spirit of the Lord is the one which oversees this change. It takes power to produce this change in each of us. It is **"even by the Spirit of the Lord"** (2 Corinthians 3:18).

When we see Jesus face to face we will fully see who Christ in us should be. There is power which comes with that. We are not just made after this power; but, we are to live by it. His power is our hope and strength. Both become available to each believer at salvation. That's the authority which was sent by God to destroy the works of the devil. This is why Jesus was sent into the world. This is why the life of Christ was given to us. This is why Christ Jesus sent us God's Spirit. 1 John 3:8 says, **"For this purpose, the Son of God was manifested, that he might destroy the works of the devil."** Only through the manifestation of our son-ship can we destroy the works of the devil. Only Christ in you can break a curse. Only finding Christ is finding power. Finding power to live is finding power to destroy the works of the devil by doing the work of God. This is why I serve the Lord. This is why He gave His people authority. This was why we were made in His image (Romans 8:29). We are being formed in life; formed in power!

Paul stated in Galatians 4:19 the words **"until Christ be formed in you."** The word **"manifested"** in 1 John 3:8 deals with this. It refers to Christ Jesus doing something only He could do. For God to form your spirit after His image is a manifestation of His power. There is no power without you being formed into His image. This is why I said your spirit is a container of the resources of God you will need for living everyday life. That's the promise of the spirit through faith (Galatians 3:14). That's the new nature which comes to your spirit man once you're born again. This is why we were restored from the fall when Adam and Eve lost dominion through their disobedience to God. This is what gives God's Spirit the right to remain upon us as believers (1 John 1:33).

Romans 8:19 says, **"For the earnest expectation of the creature waiteth for the manifestation of the sons of God."** Some other translations may say something like; the earth waits for the sons of God to manifest. That is to say, the whole of creation is waiting for Christ in us to be developed and to manifest itself for taking back dominion. The earth waits. His Word said, "the earth waits." The earth is waiting for us to manifest Christ for our son-ship. Have you ever waited on your food at a restaurant before? The earth is waiting on us to take a move in Gods direction. That's what it was made to do. It was made to submit and we were made to conquer. Dominion belongs to the body of Christ. Our spiritual position in Him (seated in heavenly places) gives us that. When we receive that position we receive the promise of His authority. If we're not walking it out it's because we haven't taken hold of His blessing. The earth is one of God's blessings (Matthew 5:5). The earth is our inheritance. The earth is waiting for us. However, we have to do our part with God in Christ first. This is where the Holy Ghost comes in. He is the one which builds us up to become what God has designed us to be. He is the one which helps you become developed as a son or daughter of God.

Live by faith

The time has come for Christ to be once again manifested in the earth. It's time for every believer to walk in the spirit and in His power. It's time to reclaim not recline. However, to reclaim dominion, a repositioning must occur. Not just in the spirit; but, in the natural as well. How can someone take authority over the earth if they don't have it over their own body? The amount of strength you have to control your own life represents the depth of authority you have in your spirit man. The authority you have in the spirit man is what provides the power to influence the spirit realm. By you taking authority over your life, you are training yourself with how to take authority over everything that may influence you. If you don't have enough power to control yourself, what makes you think you have the authority to influence something else?

The Apostle Paul said in Galatians 2:20, **"the life which I now live in the flesh I live by the faith of the Son of God."** Here we read that Paul was using the phrase **"in the flesh."** We're all in the flesh when we look at it from the natural. Paul, having a new nature through the born-again spirit canceled out the old position "the flesh" may have given him at one time. The word, flesh, from this verse is simply referring to the body, not a form of immorality. My point is this; you can't walk out dominion in and over the earth until you can do it bodily. If you don't have enough spiritual endurance to control what came out of the earth (I'm speaking of the body), then how do you ever expect to have dominion over the earth itself? Before you can take dominion over the earth, you must first take authority over what came from the earth. You'll never fully take back dominion until you take back the body. A good example of this deals with sickness. Sickness was given the right to take the body once spiritual death entered in. To hold to the idea that a part of Adam's nature remains in the body after being born again is the same as giving sickness the right to remain as well. If you believe your spirit has been resurrected from death, and the soul saved, then why over look the rights you have in the body? Do we not remain in body as we serve the cause of Christ Jesus here on earth? Do you want dominion back? Then you must take back more than the spirit and soul. You must take authority over the body!

There's something unique about Galatians 2:20. The Apostle Paul said **"I now ... live by the faith of the Son of God."** Did you catch that? In the KJV Paul didn't say, "I live by my faith in the Son of God." Did he? NO. He said "I live by the Jesus kind of faith. Wow! This takes things to a whole new level. No wonder Paul walked in such power as he did. That's why miracles happened. It wasn't Paul that was doing the work. Jesus worked through him. Can you imagine walking in the same type of faith Jesus used while on earth? For Paul to do this, he must have known Jesus personally. A personal relationship is how we find the same authority. After all, he wrote Philippians 3:10. Some folks say, *"I would love to have a moment to see into Paul's mind; to know some of what he knew and see what Paul saw."* Why stop at useless wishing? We need to by-pass Paul. Let's do what he did. We can have the mind of Christ. If we can have the mind of Christ we can have the faith of Christ; the logic of God. I don't know about some people; I just know about me. I don't want to live by my faith. I want to live by the faith of the Son of God. I want the mind of Christ. I want the logic of God. I want the Jesus faith.

> The time has come for Christ to be once again manifested in the earth. It's time for every believer to walk in the spirit and in His power. It's time to reclaim not recline.

Walk not after the flesh

Now, if your body is bound to the effects left to you from the old man, then your body would also be bound to the law of sin and death (Romans 7:23) though your spirit is not. For what is available to you through the spirit man to affect the natural side of who you are, you need to experience the same liberty in your body as in your soul and spirit. Taking hold of spirit life is taking hold of a position of dominion. Having a position of spiritual death removes this from you. The earth will only respond to the life of Christ that's working in you. The earth is not resisting us. We are resisting the earth by resisting God when we walk after "the flesh." We can't blame everything on "the flesh". We also can't blame everything on the sin nature. To believe a Christian still retains the sin nature in the body is no different than expecting the body must still maintain the same position that nature gave Adam and Eve from the beginning. The very act of gaining a sin nature was what caused Adam and Eve to lose dominion. Receiving a new nature is what will bring dominion back. For someone to assume part of the old nature resides within the body is for them to ask the question, *"What part of my spirit remains dead to God?"* To acknowledge part of Adams nature remains in the body is also the same as saying, *"I'm still of the flesh even though I'm now born again."* Furthermore, in assuming part of the sin nature dwells in the body is no different than assuming spiritual position is partly contained within the body. If the body cannot hold a spiritual position, then why do some think it can house spiritual death? (This is of course is not saying the body isn't affected by the results created by spiritual death. We know that it is.) You'll never gain back the dominion which was lost in the Garden of Eden until you first gain an understanding of life through Christ.

It is beyond me how anyone can think they have dominion over the earth if they think spiritual death is still working in their body. This is a myth built by religion and the doctrine of man. Yes, Romans 8:10 says, **"the body is dead because of sin,"** but; Christians are no longer of "the flesh", though we live in a body. Furthermore, what Paul was doing was adding more to something which he just stated. In Romans 6:6 he says, **"Knowing this, that our old man is crucified with him, that the body of sin might be destroyed, that henceforth we should not serve sin."** Do you know what **"the body of sin"** is? It is the phrase "the flesh." He wasn't talking about your physical state or body. He was talking about the effects of a dead spirit's lingering influence.

Romans 6:6 is in three parts.

1. **Our old man is crucified with him:** Death of the old man (spirit).
2. **That the body of sin might be destroyed:** Death of the flesh (soul).
3. **That henceforth we should not serve sin:** Surrender/Obedience (body).

The body was referred to as dead because it was rendered incapable of serving God by it being exposed to a dead spirit. Paul wasn't talking about destroying the physical body. Paul was talking about the damage which was inflicted upon the body and soul as a result of being spiritually dead at one time. This description isn't a literal one; only figurative. It does not exist as a natural fact. It's identifying spiritual potion. Everyone that dies in this life leaves a body behind. "The flesh" is what the dead spirit left behind. Romans 8:10 deals with where you stand before God now that you're in Christ. Through the new nature, the soul now has life as the influence to help conform us into the image of God. So, if "the flesh" isn't the body what is it? Romans 8:13 gives us the answer. **"For if ye live after the flesh, ye shall die: but if ye through the spirit do mortify the deeds of the body, ye shall live."** "The flesh" is not the body. "The flesh" is the misdeeds done in the body. The term "the flesh" refers to a state of immorality; a wrong way of thinking and taking action according to. This was engrafted within the soul and the body. Think of it as muscle memory. That's what the dead spirit left behind. It left behind what some call "the flesh."

Let's consider something from the natural. Let's take a look at the polio virus. This disease was rampant in the U.S. It reached its peak during in the 1960's. This was when a vaccination was created. If someone contracted the virus several years before, the chance that physical damage would've occurred is very high. Soon many had access to a vaccination. However, in taking it, only the virus would die. The medicine couldn't heal a twisted and broken body. Even after complete recovery the physical damage would still remain. They would no longer have the polio virus but, their physical appearance would still show the impact of the disease. The cure couldn't restore the body. All it could do was kill the virus. The damage which was done still shows the evidence that they have the look of one with the polio virus but, they're healed. What you see now is the results it left behind; a person healed yet still physically crippled. A person bound to a body affected by deaths influence.

This maybe one of the best examples I can give to help explain the sin nature and "the flesh". Just as this person was born with that disease, we're all born with a sin nature. Salvation is the administrating cure. However, the damage was done. Through salvation we're saved. We're forgiven. But, the evidence of sin's influence still remains. Just as having physical crippling effects isn't proof of polio's presents, so having temptation isn't proof of having a sin nature. Just as the virus no longer remains for those who were healed, the old nature no longer remains for those who are saved. Only the damage remains. The crippling effect of a dead spirit weakened the human body and soul. We have been restored back to God but, we still carry the damage of humanity. Salvation cured our spiritual death but, the results of life left behind a body of sin.

Now, there is a difference between being "in the flesh" and "walking after the flesh." If you're in the spirit (born again) it is possible to "walk after the flesh." However, they that are "in the flesh" cannot walk after the spirit. For someone to try to deny "the flesh" won't produce walking in the spirit, but walking in the spirit gives you the power to deny "the flesh". God doesn't give us the spirit of Christ because we deny "the flesh". Overcoming the influence of "the flesh" starts with being a living spirit. This shows us a greater revelation. Sin doesn't send someone to Hell; being spiritually dead does!

So, for someone to say they retain part of the sin nature is the same as saying they are only partly saved. This is because salvation means to be raised from spiritual death into spiritual life. For us to begin walking in dominion we must see the body can no longer hold Adam's nature any more than our spirit does. It's against the norm for a Christian to not walk in the authority their new nature provides. By gaining Adams nature in the body we would be losing dominion in the earth. Gaining the new nature is receiving the thing which gave Adam dominion in the first place. It's time to put on the new man and live.

I heard it put this way. The devil may be the god of this world (its system and function), but he is not the God of the earth. **"The earth is the Lord's, and the fullness thereof..."** (Psalms 24:1). Just as there is a difference between "the world" and "the earth," there is a difference between "the flesh" and "the body." Satan's time is running out; we through Christ now have access to ownership. It belongs to the Church. In the end, when Christ Jesus returns, we will see our enemy fall and full order begin. Full dominion is coming soon. Those who have the life of Christ as an indwelling nature will one day enjoy it.

God's tabernacle is Holy

When is the Church going to awaken to a deeper level of God's truth? We need a greater understanding of Christ in the last days. His people perish for lack of knowledge. I thought the Church knew the body was the temple of the Lord. Why would anyone want to think of the body as the temple of the Lord and a container of the old nature? If the old man is dead, why think that his nature lives on? That's an insult to the work of Christ to assume such a thing in the first place. I brought that up because I've heard so many speak as though the Word is talking about your spirit man being His temple. This sounds good, but what is written? This has been discussed in different places throughout the New Testament. Paul wrote about it in 1 Corinthians 3:16-17 and also in 1 Corinthians 6:12-20. **"Know ye not that "your body" is the temple of the Holy Ghost"** (1 Corinthians 6:15). Here he just said the body is God's temple. This is what Peter had to say. **"Yea, I think it meet, as long as I am in this tabernacle, to stir you up by putting you in remembrance; Knowing that shortly I must put off this my tabernacle, even as our Lord Jesus Christ hath shewed me."** (2 Peter 1:13-14). Peter just referred to his body as being a tabernacle. The body has been given an evil report because of the misuse of the term "the flesh." It comes through those who can't control themselves or who simply have not yet learned there's more. Do you think God wants to live in a house of corruption? The body is part of God's dwelling place. What makes you think it still holds corruption? I think I may know why. It's by two ideas. The first idea has come through wrong teaching and a miss-interpretation of God's Word. Some study God's Word through observation of the body instead of observing the influence of "the flesh" through the study of God's

> Just as there is a difference between "the world" and "the earth," there is a difference between "the flesh" and "the body." Satan's time is running out; we through Christ now have access to ownership. It belongs to the Church.

Word. In other words, they use their life as the interruption of God's Word. What we should do is use the Word of God as the interpretation of our life. The second comes with us knowing the body is human. Being human in body doesn't identify who you are. Who you are is identified by your spiritual position. It's not who Adam was. It's about who Christ Jesus is! We must not only cleanse ourselves of all filthiness in spirit, but we must do it in body as well (2 Corinthians 7:1) As long as we are receptive to this world's influences we will be exposed to temptation. From time to time we all have felt its deceptive pull. That makes it all the more important to remember the body, along with the spirit and soul, belong to the Lord.

> Being glorified in the earth was Him taking back the same position Adam lost. Spiritual authority changed hands that day. He was doing this not for Himself, but for the Church. Christ Jesus left. We have access to that authority now. The only real power the devil has is the control people hand over to him through their disobedience to God.

Know ye not that ye are the temple of God, and that the Spirit of God dwelleth in you? If any man defile the temple of God, him shall God destroy; for the temple of God is holy, which temple ye are." – 1 Corinthians 3:16-17

Those that have an old mindset about "the flesh' will most likely find these truths contradictory to the Word. Let's consider Ephesians 6:12 for a moment. **"For we wrestle not against flesh and blood…"** Did you not deduce this statement also included where you stand before God? Are you not made of flesh and blood? You cannot analyze a spiritual position through observation of "the flesh". For me to blame "the flesh" would be no different than trying to create an excuse for failure. I'm not looking for that. I want His liberty. In order to walk by faith one must disregard the position once birthed in the body back when the spirit man was dead before God. I don't have all the answers to explain the human body versus "the flesh." However, I do have one answer. That's Jesus. If we have Him in spirit form then we're not in "the flesh" (Romans 8:9). If we're going to hold to more of the things of the spirit of life than in times past, we must look deeper at who we are in Christ. A carnal mind will always find a place to fit in where "the flesh" stands.

No one will successfully establish their life as a Christian if it's after the mindset of "the flesh". I'm looking to find fulfillment as a living spirit. This may be why I have a unique focus. The cup of my life is half full, not half empty.

Please don't criticize or judge me for my ability to reason out God's Word as I'm able. You must understand when your focus is coming out of the spirit man you see a big difference between "the flesh" and "the body." I have determined not to miss more of Christ Jesus because of being limited in my knowledge of God. I have to stay open-minded if I'm going to see and understand deeper truth. I have determined to no longer live in Egypt by still living with that mind-set. I now have a stronger passion for more of God than I had just a few years ago as well as more knowledge of who I am in Christ. I know what I've seen. I know His power can do anything as long as I have the faith in me to take the necessary stand.

Give no place to the devil

There are people who still think of the devil as having power. I suppose it all depends on how you're looking at it. This power is something that's relative. It depends on how you see things. Just before Christ Jesus was taken to heaven He said to His disciples, *"All power is given unto me in heaven and in earth."* (Matthew 28:18). That's all we need to know. The word power here deals with Jesus being glorified in the earth. Being glorified in the earth was Him taking back the same position Adam lost. Spiritual authority changed hands that day. He was doing this not for Himself, but for the Church. Christ Jesus left. We have access to that authority now. The only real power the devil has is the control people hand over to him through their disobedience to God. If you don't want the devil to dominate any part of your life, then don't surrender anything over to him (James 4:7-8). Stop giving him room to do his work. Don't expect the devil to leave you alone if you're not willing to leave the world alone. We must above all else submit to God. The devil is very good when it comes to finding our weaknesses. Watching how we respond to the world gives him the information he needs. Everything of the world which remains in our life that we haven't yet taken dominion over is something the devil can access and use one day to control us. Too many times the love for the things of the world controls us instead of the other way around. Instead of a person taking dominion over it, it takes dominion over them. This is where the devil finds his power. If he can control what's attached to us, he can control us. Why would you want to surrender to the world when you can have liberty over that influence through Christ? You can't submit your life to the control of the world and be free at the same time.

I know there's a real devil. Yet, I understand nearly all his power is limited to his ability to influence me. The statement, *"Every new level brings a new devil,"* may be true. I also know his power to control me is limited to the ability he has to control what's still attached to me. Now don't get me wrong. I'm not someone which ignores the fact that the devil is still at work. Furthermore, I'm not saying he doesn't pull or push against me. I'm just looking towards another factor. It involves my character as a real Christian. I think some Christian's act like they know more about the devil and his work than they know of God and His. Those people may know more about failure than success. Yet, our focus should be on a relationship with our Father in heaven. How we relate to the world will show others where we stand. How we relate to and respond to the world is very important. We must study our reactions to the world's influences and where we stand with God when they reoccur.

I know myself. I have seen where I've fallen before God. For me to continue to respond that way would be pure neglect on my part where new spiritual growth is concerned. If someone falls into the same trap over and over again, one might think they would have the awareness to recognize something's wrong. If we are willing to deal with the handles the devil has placed in us, along with those the world brings, we'll be much closer to the liberty God has for us. Jesus paid it all. You don't have to defeat the devil. Christ Jesus has already done that. All we have to do is die to self so Christ in us can live.

Have you made room for the devil in your life? Are you welcoming the world and don't know it? I have a cat and every night all her food would disappear. In the act of leaving food outside, the other animals in the area have learned it's there. They won't leave as long as there's food available. It won't matter if I hide and watch for the opportune moment to frighten them off. As long as I keep leaving out food they will keep coming back night after night. In order to get rid of them I had to stop leaving food out. That provision was the same as a welcome to them. My point is this, as long as I kept feeding them, they kept coming back. In the same way, if the devil or the world keeps revisiting your life, it's because you're still putting out the food. That's the same as making room for it. What you feed will grow stronger. It's a surprising thing to see how little ground the devil needs to get his foot in the door of our life. All it may take is a slight opportunity; a small gap to gain access.

I have known people who've allowed the devil in. Getting rid of him can be as hard as trying to kill off an infestation of some kind in your house. Just like bugs, the devil likes to find small places to hide. These hidden places are strongholds. The last thing anyone needs is for the devil to wait until you're in the spotlight then activate something hidden in you which you did not know of. I don't want the devil to reserve a place in me. That's allowing him to control my spiritual growth. All he needs to do to stop me from going deeper is to pull on what he still controls. If the enemy can control what's in you, he can control you. Having liberty starts with searching one's heart and mind to find how the enemy was and keeps getting in. Secondly, we need to examine the condition of our soul. Between one and ten, where do you rate yourself before the Ten Commandments? How do you measure up to the fruits of the Spirit? In order to advance in the kingdom we need to develop the right charter. We need to find where the world and the enemy is getting in. We need to recover that ground back. The fight is part of having dominion. Through poor management and a lack of surrender to the Lord, we make ourselves vulnerable to the world while strengthening its hold over us at the same time.

Let's look deeper into the topic of attachments. Matthew 16:24 reports, **"If any man will come after me, let him deny himself, and take up his cross, and follow me."** In this verse, the word **"himself"** has a special meaning for me. Worldly things like anger, unforgiveness, fear, greed, lust, substances abuse, pride, along with a long list of other things, are self-centered in nature. This is the self part you are to deny. Someone would have to be in denial of the truth to not deny "the flesh". When we accept self, we deny Christ. Someone would have to turn away from the spirit side of who they are to accept self. Self is a reflection of the world. The born again spirit is a reflection of Christ. You're not losing the fun life can bring. Your life is being saved from the very things which will rob you of life. We are not just conquerors, we are more than conquerors. We must learn how to respond more to God than to what's in the world. To do this right one needs a deeper relationship with the Father. This is so you can see when it's Christ in you doing the pulling instead of the world or what's coming out of the self part of you which needs to be denied. I have decided to no longer use what the world offers as an excuse. It's time to overcome it by being activated in the spirit man. It's time for more change. It's time to give God more room in our life.

> I think some Christian's act like they know more about the devil and his work than they know of God and His. Those people may know more about failure than success. Our focus should be on a relationship with our Father in heaven. How we relate to the world will show others where we stand.

Surrendering to God deals with more than managing your mindset by how you reason things out or how you feel. One must not overlook the external, such as dealing with people and money. Dominion involves all that you have the potential to influence. This comes by actions which are designed to inspire others or by an intention to deceive and break down another's willpower to the point of control. That's how the devil gains power over others. By gaining the power to influence everything they control by controlling them. Most people can't see the enemy is involved. Many times they think it's who they are that's bringing wrong motives. If the devil can deceive us by causing us to be a wrong influence, instead of being one for the kingdom of God, then he's stealing back another part of the dominion which is ours through Christ Jesus. We are the one that's giving the devil his power just as Adam and Eve once did. Jesus took it back through His life on earth, death on the cross, and resurrection from the grave. So, let's keep dominion where it belongs. Let's keep it in the hands of God's servants and followers. Dominion belongs to us who know Christ and believe. However, just because someone has a relationship with God as a child to a Father, does not mean they know what belongs to them.

> Dominion involves all that you have the potential to influence. This comes by actions which are designed to inspire others or by an intention to deceive and break down another's willpower to the point of control. That's how the devil gains power over others. By gaining the power to influence everything they control by controlling them.

Over the years I've come to see change is the key to spiritual strength. Real change comes to my life by a daily walk with the Lord. This changes who I am as a person. First, it's with who I am as a living spirit. After that comes my mind, will, and emotions or my soul. Then finally how I see myself where the body stands. The secret to any success I have comes through the knowledge of Christ and of God that relates to all three. One must also consider how the influence of the world will affect all three. I also know how important having a relationship with God can be. I consider having a relationship with God my number one core value. In Him, I have found the true meaning of love. Along with that comes Christ in me: my new nature. Christ is my hope. In addition to these two faith has become my logic. These three virtues are Faith, hope, and love. Under the influence of these three, the outcome for my life has been one of power instead of weakness.

CHAPTER 20
WALK IN SPIRIT; WALK IN POWER

WHEN THE APOSTLE PAUL STARTED CALLING OUT THE SIN OF THE CHURCH IN HIS first letter to the Corinthians, he stated, **"and my spirit, with the power of our Lord Jesus Christ"** (1 Cor. 5:4). When this phrase caught my attention, it helped to reinforce my understanding that there is a difference between my spirit and the supply of the spirit of Christ Jesus. Allow me to recap a few facts concerning the spirit man. It is possible to have a spirit and not be born again. That's a spirit which is dead to God. The spirit man, one which has been raised to new life through salvation, is born again. This is sometimes called the second birth or new birth. This is a spirit that's made alive to God. In addition to that, what Paul said here also included the power of Christ. This power is the authority of the kingdom which is available to every believer. That is why we find the words **"in power"** in this verse, **"For the kingdom of God is not in word, but in power"** (1 Corinthians 4:20). If we look back to 1 Corinthians 1:24 we learned that Christ is the power of God. It dealt with what having a living spirit can provide for you. My focus for this book is to introduce the Spirit of God as I have seen Him in my life personally and how He has aided me in spiritually developing who I am after the image of Christ. Our spirit deals with the image of God that's formed in us at salvation. The power deals with His resurrection and what comes to us because of it.

In John 5:30 Jesus says, **"I can of mine own self do nothing."** Christ Jesus expressed His trust and submission to the Father. He recognized the Father as His source for all which was being done. I believe in every work He did, He did it as a man. Not as God. I can say that because He was continually giving God the credit. I also can say this because He knew that was the only way we would be able to serve Him. We can do nothing of ourselves. The Holy Spirit may anoint you, but Jesus still does the work. Power comes to us only through having the spirit of Christ. That's what the Apostle Paul meant when he said, **"I can do all things through Christ who strengthens me."** (Philippians 4:13). He was speaking of having a spirit of power in Christ. That's the spirit which is no longer born of Adam but is now born of Christ Jesus. Without the spirit of Christ or the new nature, we can do nothing for the kingdom.

In finding how to live out of Christ in you, you will experience what the Spirit of God has the power to do. It's Christ in you that God needs to use. If the Holy Ghost takes hold of anything in you, it will be that which has been changed from death to life. That life is the new nature. Without this, there is nothing in you God can use. This is why Paul's focus was on Christ Jesus so much. He knew Christ must become a living-working factor in him daily to truly be used by the Lord. He knew this was the key to kingdom authority. This is why Paul said in Ephesians 4:13, **"Till we all come in the unity of the faith, and of the knowledge of the Son of God, unto a perfect man, unto the measure of the stature of the fullness of Christ."** The word **"perfect"** here means to be complete or developed. To become more developed, we have to first gain the knowledge of who Christ in us is and walk by it daily. For that, we will need the Word of God and an interactive relationship with Him. Secondly, we need to be baptized in the power of the Holy Ghost. Here is what I heard from God about His Spirit and His baptism; it was that I was an incomplete Christian without His presence and the work of His Spirit at work in and through my life. I think all who are born again have the fellowship of God's Spirit to one degree or another. But, is His life growing in you? Do you have the working of His power? There is a difference between the power of Christ and the anointing of the Holy Ghost. We need the anointing just as much as we need Christ. The knowledge of Christ will give each of us a measure of faith and a portion of power. I equate this authority towards dominion. The knowledge of God gives us the ability to yield to Him and to walk it out. I've come to see the knowledge of God pertains to faith. The knowledge of Christ is to know, understand, and serve the image of God you now have as a born again believer. The Holy Ghost can activate Christ in you in ways which you can't by yourself. The supply that comes from both is what enables us to become developed into the stature of the fullness of Christ. The Holy Ghost and the power of Christ will equip us in both. So, what are you, as a part of His body, doing to take hold of the measure of the fullness of the stature of Christ and the power of the Holy Ghost?

Why was the Apostle Paul so determined for the Corinthian Church to only know him after Christ and Him crucified (1 Corinthians 2:2)? In 1 Corinthians 14: 18 Paul said, **"I thank my God, I speak with tongues more than ye all."** This sounds like a contradiction. I wanted to point to this because many churches enjoy being identified as being Spirit-filled. They like the prestige. This, however, may be based on the self-perception of their achievements or spiritual quality. Yet, there are others which enjoy only being recognized as salvation preaching churches. They sometimes fit the same definition. This is pride. Don't misunderstand my approach to this: or rather to say reproach. I'm looking for the balance which exists between the two. I'm searching it out because I want to be all I can be for God. The fullness of Christ in you won't come from a one-sided viewpoint. I'm not telling you I think Paul, or anyone else, was becoming as Jesus. Jesus is in heaven. However, the Bible does say we are being conformed into the image of Christ after our spirit man. Romans 8:29 says, **"For whom he did foreknow, he also did predestine to be conformed to the image of his Son."** We're not supposed to look like the Holy Ghost. God's Spirit is not the Son of God. The Holy Ghost doesn't cry Abba-Father. He is God in Spirit form. Believers are to have a spirit after the form of the Son of God. That's why Paul said what he did. We don't have to focus on the Holy Ghost all the time if our focus is on Christ Jesus properly. After all, that's what the Holy Ghost is focused on. In John 16:13 Christ Jesus tells us He (the Holy Ghost) will not speak of Himself. His ministry is to speak of and confirm Christ Jesus. One of His jobs is to activate Christ in you. The Holy Ghost is not anointing you just because you're you. His job is to anoint the Christ that's working in you.

Thinking about Christ living in and through me brought something back to my recollection. Some time ago I stopped by my parent's house for a visit. While there I found myself standing by a kitchen cabinet. My dad was cooking dinner. Without taking thought of my actions, I opened one of the drawers and looked through the different objects. It was a junk drawer. I think every house has one. There were still things in it I put there myself. All of a sudden, my mom walks in and shouts, *"Get out of my drawer; you don't live here anymore. Remember?"* She wasn't angry with me. The grin on her face proved it. She then said, *"Whenever daddy would come over to eat with us he would do the same thing."* That's when she realized what she just said. *"You're acting just like him."* My mother dearly loved granddaddy. Though he passed away many years ago, part of him was still here living through me. I'm not him. Yet, through my actions, she saw a little of her father in me. Christ Jesus also said if you've seen Him, you've seen the Father (John 14:9-10). When people look at you, do they see the Son? You may be the only Jesus some people will ever see.

In John chapter 16:12 Jesus said, **"I have yet many things to say unto you, but ye cannot bear them now."** As the time of the end comes closer, the Church gains back more of the knowledge of Christ and of God. This may have begun when Martin Luther saw the truth of **"for grace you are saved through faith."** It wasn't called the dark ages for nothing. Now, more light has come to the Church because of understanding more truth. The Spirit of God has shown me some things. Yet, there are still many more Christians which do not know them. For us to increase in the spirit, our understanding must grow.

"Howbeit when he, the Spirit of truth, is come, he will guide you into all truth: for he shall not speak of himself; but whatsoever he shall hear, that shall he speak: and he will show you things to come." (John 16:13) I know there is more we don't yet understand, much more. Jesus said in verse 15, **"he shall take of mine, and shall shew it unto you."** The more of Jesus you want, the more of the Holy Ghost you will get. In addition to this, he was not only saying He would give us the truth by giving us Jesus; but, the Holy Ghost would show us what the Father was now doing in the earth. This could be why parts of the body of Christ struggle. It's because they lack these two things. They lack being equipped in the power of Christ with the baptism of God's Spirit and they do not see what the Father is doing. In this, we have the Father, the Son, and the Holy Ghost.

Dominion starts with Christ

I know many who call themselves Christian which lack the knowledge of who they are in Christ. They focus on the rapture as though there's nothing here left to do. I'm not against the rapture. No. I believe in it. They're the ones which aren't ready for it, and I'll tell you why. We all know the Bible has been saying for around two thousand years we're in the last days. Two thousand years is a whole lot of last days, don't you think? It seems like something is missing. I think Acts 3:20-21 may hold the key to guiding our understanding of this. **"And he shall send Jesus Christ, which before was preached unto you: Whom the heavens must receive until the times of restitution of all things, which God hath spoken by the mouth of all his holy prophets since the world began."** The Apostle Peter said the heavens had to take Christ Jesus. I understand why He had to leave. We know Christ Jesus said the Holy Ghost couldn't come until He was taken. These verses identify the rapture of Jesus. Thus, they point directly to details concerning our rapture. This is something which needs to be pointed out. Peter said Christ Jesus was taken up until something happens. God the Father is holding back His Son until the times of restitution of all things first takes place. After all, God's holy prophets have been speaking of this since the very beginning. So, whatever it is, it took place when the world began. Can you think of what that might be? It was the fall of man. This was when Adam and Eve disobeyed God by taking the forbidden fruit. This act hurled mankind into spiritual death. The loss of fellowship with God is not the only thing that happened. So, what's missing? Dominion was lost. What if the rapture doesn't come until, we the Church, rise up in the same power Christ and the Apostles once walked in. What if taking back dominion is the key to unlocking heaven's doors?

> *"And he shall send Jesus Christ, which before was preached unto you: Whom the heavens must receive until the times of restitution of all things, which God hath spoken by the mouth of all his holy prophets since the world began."* Acts 3:20-21

I know the one world order is coming. I know the evil one will dominate all he can access. When I refer to our dominion, I'm not looking at it the same way as it has been looked at in times past. This was why some of the Jews couldn't see Christ Jesus as the Messiah. It was in their minds God would take control in the natural to take it by force. This is not the dominion Christ was bringing back. Control is not dominion! The end of all things as we know it is coming. The devil will reveal his antichrist. Full demonic control of the world's system and its function will be a reality one day. This control is the closest thing to him taking dominion as he's going to have. This is his counter-part to true dominion. This focus is on the natural more than the supernatural. True dominion starts with taking back spiritual ground. Satan's control is no more a real picture of dominion than his antichrist is a model of the image of God. Real dominion is what we have if we are in Christ. It's not what we get by who we are in the world. It's about who we are in Christ. However, most Christians have never begun to know the image of Christ that's formed in their spirit through salvation or know the power that image holds and what it's capable of doing. I believe having dominion starts with that because, it starts with Christ. If the prophecy found in Acts chapter 3 is true then God may not release Christ Jesus to bring about our rapture until the Church becomes developed in their spiritual position for the manifestation of their sonship. I think this is the very thing which is holding back the rapture. If we are going to see it come, we need to become developed in who we are in Christ. Only the Father knows how much longer it may be if the Church doesn't take charge of themselves and step into the work God started releasing to the Church back in the book of Acts.

Conclusion

Over the years as I've grown spiritually, I could see more or less fifty different major biblical revelations. Each truth was foundational in building my life as it built my spirit man after the image of God in Christ. I could see a timeline was involved as it all came together around June 2012. That was when I was shown the first book. As I began to write the vision down, many things became plain. Like why God arranged me to stay single for so long, why I saw God's glory, and why I've come to know these truths while they have been overlooked by others. After I began to put the first book together, I no longer saw many truths. I found myself seeing only one. Before, I didn't see how they all might fit together. There were times, during those years, when I wasn't sure I was still following the call of God. Now I see His call was what carried me through.

When I look back over the years of 1997 to now, I notice how God moved in my life in waves. There were, amazingly enough, three waves in all. First, there was my dedication back to Him at the beginning of 1997. This introduced Christ and how having a relationship with God was so important. This identified God as my source. Then, there was everything which took place in 1999. I saw how this introduced the Holy Ghost. His power became a force for strength. The last season started when I joined up with my mentor in January of 2003. This was setting my course. Each wave included more spiritual growth than the one before it. I come to understand they were seasons of change and preparation. I also have seen waves of threes on a smaller scale. There were three waves of introduction into the baptism of the Holy Spirit. Three waves where others recognized my call. Three times where others saw the hand of God upon my life before Pastor Hinn called me out on it. Then, there were three outpourings of power at the last conference. Have you ever wondered why God may often move in waves of three? Is it because there are three realms? Maybe the first impartation marks the sovereignty of God. Perhaps the second wave releases God's authority in the second realm where spiritual warfare takes place. After all, we are seated in heavenly places. What if the third impartation establishes it as a faith law in the natural? I'm not sure. However, I still see God bring advancement in waves of threes in the lives of others around me.

Another thing I've noticed about the timeline was it started in January of 1997 and continued until I was called to preach. That was around two years and nine months. I now see the same timeline had just occurred again from when I saw the first book "Dead to Sin" and began to write it, to the time when it was put into print. There was also another occurrence; I was shown the name of this ministry. From the time I got His call to write, to seeing the name of this ministry, that same timeline was introduced. It marked a starting point, then a place of completion. With this, I see a new season beginning in my life. I guess you could call it the start of a second cycle of development. At the end of this first cycle, I saw certain things in my life that God was working on come to a place of maturity. Now I see Him introducing new change for a new life and level of His power.

I know now that everything in this ministry and my life, from here on out, will in some way either connect to or fall back on one truth. This one truth is the revelation I have mentioned at the start of this book. It is Philippians 3:10, **"That I may know Him and the power of His resurrection."** This is why I've chosen to presented the ministry logo as I have. I can truly say there's nothing in this life more important than finding out all we can about this and growing in it. It has the power to change everything for you as its changing things for me. As I think back, I could've walked past the framed parchment that day so long ago. What if that was the case? Would I be doing what I'm doing now? Would God have given this revelation and ministry to another person? No matter. I have come to see God really does know the end of our life from the beginning. He shapes our end. I also know every believer thinks from time to time, *"Lord, where are you right now? Have I missed you?"* I know we miss God from time to time. We're not yet made perfect; but, there is peace in knowing that He is perfect. I thank God for Christ and for the Holy Ghost. I don't know what the future holds, but I know who's holding me. I know His hand is on my life. I have also learned enough about Him to say, if your reading this book, His hand is also upon you. He did His part by sending His Son and His Spirit. We do our part by accepting and surrendering the life we now have to Him. After all, how can Christ be in you without a yielding to Him first taking place? And, how can the Holy Ghost use you without Christ being a working factor in your life? For Christ to live through us, we must stop living for ourselves. We need to live for God. It will take this if we're ever going to see Him move once again as He did in the book of Acts. Is this what you want to see? Do you not want to know the truth? Don't you want to see things as they are in your life change? I think you do. Having an interactive relationship in place is required for this. You can know Him. You can experience His power. He wants to reveal His glory to you. He wants to use you. It's time for the sons and daughters of God to manifest Christ. It's time for the power of God to be released. It's time for the Church to arise.

It's time for righteous change. It's time to do the work of God by walking in spirit and in power.

"Now the God of peace, that brought again from the dead our Lord Jesus, that great shepherd of the sheep, through the blood of the everlasting covenant, make you perfect in every good work to do his will, working in you that which is well-pleasing in His sight, through Jesus Christ; to whom be glory forever and ever. Amen." – Hebrews 13:20-21

About the Author

Marty Sudderth is the founder of Finding Power to Live Ministries.

He is married to Kayla Howard Sudderth and has one son, Michael, and two daughters, Amelia and Audrey.

Marty was raised in a Southern Baptist Church, he received the Lord is his personal Savior at the age of 8. He experienced God's Revival fire at the age of 24 and was called into ministry two years later.

Marty attended Truett McConnell Bible College and has preached in five different denominations and three trans-denominational ministries.

His Christian service has included usher, door-to-door Ministry, deacon, nursing home ministry, campground ministry, street ministry, food drive ministry, altar worker coordinator, pastoral Elder, children's church pastor, singles pastor, church van driver, and evangelist.

Personally, Marty is a man of integrity, honest, sober, holding to the character of meekness and gentleness. He is a man that keeps his word. It has been said that he has a heart of gold. Alongside Intimacy in relationship with God, faith hope and love are his core values. Marty believes the Bible is the inspired Word of God. He also believes in the body of Christ, the organized Church, and in bridging gaps between denominations.

Contact information:

www.findingpowertoliveministries.com
findingpowertolive@gmail.com

www.ingramcontent.com/pod-product-compliance
Lightning Source LLC
Chambersburg PA
CBHW070454100426
42743CB00010B/1610